Successful Family Ties

Successful FAMILY TIES

RON BALL

Tyndale House
Publishers, Inc.
Wheaton, Illinois

Scripture marked TLB is taken from *The Living Bible,* © 1971 by Tyndale House Publishers, Inc., Wheaton, Illinois. Scripture marked NIV is taken from *The Holy Bible,* New International Version, © 1978 by New York International Bible Society. Scripture marked NASB is taken from *The New American Standard Bible,* © 1960, 1962, 1963, 1968, 1971, 1972, 1973 by The Lockman Foundation. Scripture marked NKJV is taken from *The Holy Bible,* New King James Version, © 1979, 1980, 1982 by Thomas Nelson, Inc., Publishers.

First printing, August 1988
Library of Congress Catalog Card Number 88-51049
ISBN 0-8423-6602-4
© 1988 by Ron Ball
Printed in the United States of America

To Amy and Birdie
The women we love

CONTENTS

PREFACE

When my children were very young and my marriage was just as new, there weren't many books available on the subjects covered in this one. However, during the course of my growing years until this day I have faced many challenges—as do most successful people—and I've learned a great deal from them. My business has provided the atmosphere and environment for "developing right relationships for lasting success." It's those lasting relationships that are the glue and meaning to life and yet they are more absent today than possibly at any other time in history.

We have more stress to deal with today than we did twenty or thirty years ago, and that increased stress is more intense and complicated—all the more reason to develop and restore relationships with those you love and those who are important to you. In past generations, the answers to life's questions concerning the family could be reasoned out a little easier with common sense, but today the answers seem to be beyond the reach of young adults, newlyweds, and long-time parents alike.

Those answers are within reach now, as you read and reread Ron Ball's book *Successful Family Ties*. Ron is a friend and associate whose principles are proven and whose words are true. I wish someone had given me a book like this one twenty or thirty years ago. This book will answer your questions and provide you with the knowledge to build those relationships, with chapters such as "Pressure from Parents," "Commitment to Communication," and "Positive Thinking and Negative People."

I know that once you exercise this knowledge you will have the skills, attitudes, discipline, and desire needed to reach your goals, fulfill your dreams, and therefore change the world around you.

Above all, whether you're working to build a successful family or a successful business, remember this Scripture from Proverbs by which I have lived my life: "In everything you do, put God first, and he will direct you and crown your efforts with success" (3:6, TLB).

Dexter Yager, Sr.
President and CEO of Yager Enterprises
Charlotte, North Carolina

INTRODUCTION

On a September afternoon in 1985, my wife, Amy, and I had our first in-depth encounter with Dexter and Birdie Yager. We already knew their reputations as Christian business leaders. We also knew they had built their great success and wealth through a network of business interests. Our visit was insightful and exciting as Dex and I realized we had many goals in common. We were both committed to communicate Jesus Christ, and we shared the conviction that everyone should be impacted by God's principles on balanced success: wise money management, personal integrity, and the priority of the family. An important relationship was born.

Dexter has taught me to make theory practical, and he has fed my mind with much of the material in this book. It is not my book; it is our book. His practical wisdom has influenced every chapter. We have traveled and spoken together, prayed and dreamed together. He has counseled and taught, and I have listened and learned.

Much of this book is based on his input. God has used this knowledge to bring me to whatever level of understanding I now have. God has also used this relationship to develop my concern for the problems of the family in this generation. It is Dexter's and my hope that this book will speak to problems you may be facing and that it will give you the tools and the hope on which to build success in your family.

I was in Atlanta recently visiting friends, and while I was there they took me to see a lovely, Williamsburg-style house listed for sale. They had been encouraging me for some time to buy a house in their neighborhood because of our friendship and because of the opportunities. Before we saw the house, my friends said to me, "The owner has just divorced and he may not want to discuss that aspect of his life. He's probably under stress, so be aware of that." We entered the house, and my friends introduced me to the neighbor. He seemed to be a very pleasant gentleman. He was well spoken and showed us around the house graciously, but I did detect something very serious as I talked with him. His eyes, body mannerisms, tone of voice—everything indicated he was under severe strain. As we made our way upstairs, I met the man's teenage son. He, too, was under tremendous pressure. I was so taken by the needs of this man and his son that I forgot all about the house. I told my friends how important it was for us to pray for this man and his wife and his son, asking God to help them through this crisis.

Three days later, I was with another couple eating dinner. The man opened up the afternoon newspaper, and said, "Look at this! Here is a picture of a man we know. We've gone to church with him for years! A few years ago, he had a severe illness. We prayed with him, and asked the Lord to touch him and heal him, and that's exactly what happened. God healed this man. It was miraculous! His marriage was strengthened through the event, and his wife and he became very close." And then he said, "The newspaper says he has just divorced his wife and married someone else. I don't understand what happened. They supported each other through a time of great crisis. I wonder what went wrong." My friend threw the paper down and looked at me in disgust. "What can we do? God did a miracle in this man's life. What went wrong?"

I have experienced situations like these numerous times, so often that I have come to expect them. I do not want to be pessimistic, but everywhere I go, people come to me with great needs in the areas of family, marriage, and relationships. We are living in a generation that is facing tremendous pressure in this regard—a generation of immaturity and irresponsibility, a generation in which self-centeredness seems to dominate relationships. There is an absence of practical wisdom that must be corrected. And that is my purpose in researching and presenting this material to you: to give you some practical, biblically based wisdom to help you overcome the problems you face in your relationships.

My wife, Amy, and I have been married for more than fifteen years, and we have gone through the various struggles and adjustments most people have. We have prayed and worked through problems and overcome crises with God's help, and we are aware that the principles of the Bible do work in a marriage. The more I encounter men and women such as the ones I have just described, the more I am convinced of the great need of this generation for God's help in marriage and family relationships. I am also convinced that there must be a return to commonsense, biblical living.

Clarence Eldridge, a former senior vice-president of the Campbell Soup Company, said, "One word that characterizes the ideal relationship is permanence. If permanency is to be achieved, it must be in the minds of the parties from the very beginning. It must be deliberately and consciously built into the relationship" [David Ogilvy, *Confessions of an Advertising Man* (Atheneum, 1980), 74]. And that, of course, is the fundamental principle that guides everything I say about marriage. It is a biblical principle. Jesus said, "They are no longer two, but one. Therefore what God has joined together, let man not separate" (Matthew 19:6, NIV). In that amazing moment when Adam looked at the first woman, Eve, he said, "This is now bone of my bones and flesh of my flesh; she shall be called 'woman' for she was taken out of man" (Genesis 3:23, NIV). There is a mysterious, intangible moment when Adam knows there is something significant happening, a potential completion with this woman that needs to be permanent for him to be who he can be and who he needs to be as a human being. I believe that should guide our understanding of marriage: permanence. I am a believer in Scripture; I believe the Bible is the inerrant word of God, and I am committed to that intellectually, emotionally, spiritually, and professionally. And I believe that the biblical principles stated within the Word of God, especially the principle of permanence, should be the foundation of every marriage relationship.

Amy and I have had to adjust in every area covered in this book. We have worked through sexual ups and downs and through selfishness—that material came out of my own problems in being self-centered with her. We have struggled to build a right relationship, adjusted to pressure from our parents, fought over communication problems, and overcome negative people. The solutions have come through studying the Bible and through broad reading in areas of sociology, psychology, and training I had in college, seminary, and graduate school. But most of all this material comes from our personal experiences and the hundreds of counseling situations I have been in as a pastor. I was a pastor twice and also an evangelist. I did about four hundred crusade meetings and rallies over five years in which I worked with Charles Stanley at First Baptist Church in Atlanta—one of the most wonderful experiences of my life. In the last few years I have spoken for business conventions in different parts of the world to many people who do not know Jesus Christ and even at times do not share the biblical values and principles that I believe are vital to a successful life.

By the tremendous response I've received I know this material is something people need to hear. I hope you will learn as I have learned that God's principles always work. You need to work them with honesty, work them with maturity and commitment; you need to work them sometimes with great courage, but you must work these principles if you are going to have God's positive and enjoyable results in your marriage and your relationships. I am thankful for the opportunity to relive much of this journey with you. My wife and I are excited at this opportunity for God to communicate with you vital principles of human relationships that make marriage what it can be and what you really want it to be: the most deeply fulfilling of all human arrangements and all human situations.

ONE
RIGHT RELATIONSHIPS

When I first met my wife, Amy, I was taken with her. She was attractive, I loved her personality, and I was captured by her presence. She also had a deep and exciting commitment to Jesus Christ. But Amy was also very popular on the campus of the small college we attended, and it was difficult to get a date with her. We were merely casual acquaintances for two years. By the time I was a graduating senior, she was getting ready to begin her junior year. I had decided to go to summer school to finish my final courses for graduation because it gave me more time to do what I loved most, which was speaking in small churches and at church crusade meetings in the area.

I arrived on campus for summer school about three or four o'clock in the morning, having just finished a crusade meeting near Pittsburgh, Pennsylvania. I was very tired, but slept only two hours and got up to get some breakfast to be ready for the day. As I walked toward the cafeteria, I made a detour to the campus post office to mail a letter. And there was Amy. Six o'clock in the morning. I was captured again by the same emotions I had felt two years before. We spoke for a moment, and I thought, *It's going to be a great summer! God must have done this!* I was eager now for summer school.

I found opportunities to speak with her and waited for her in different places all over campus. I did everything I could to make sure she noticed me. I even arranged through a friend of mine to have Amy come as a vocalist on two crusade meetings at which I was speaking. I have to admit I had some mixed motives. I wanted God to put together the right team, but I wanted Amy to be a part of that team. She sang and I spoke, and we had a wonderful time.

Finally, I decided I had worked up the nerve to ask her out, but it turned out to be much more difficult than I had anticipated. I said, "Amy, could I talk to you for a few minutes?" She said, "Sure," so we went outside and started to walk and walk and walk. I stalled and tried to come up with all kinds of topics for discussion because I was thinking, *Why would she say yes to a date with me when she has so many dates already?* After more than forty-five minutes of circuitous conversation, I looked at her and said, "Amy, would you like to go out with me Friday night?" And she said, "Why, yes, I would love to." And I thought, *Oh, wow, this is great!*

My heart did all of the usual leaps. But I managed to say, "Great! Friday night!"

On Friday night I picked her up, and I was actually more nervous than when I had asked her out. I had decided to pack the date with activity. I thought if we did enough, then I could get through the evening without making a fool of myself, and I just might have a chance for another date. So, we went bowling, we played golf, we got some dessert, we walked around. We had a lovely time, but there was one incident that really had a profound—and I don't use that word lightly—effect on me. We were driving down the highway. It was a warm summer night in late June, and the sun was just setting in front of us. It was beautiful, and Amy began to sing Scripture songs. I was very quiet, and God began to deeply touch my heart. Here was a young woman whose personality excited, challenged, and stretched me and whose commitment to Jesus Christ was now inspiring me. I thought, *I want to know her better.*

I am very romantic by nature—sentimental, emotional. I have highs and lows and moods. All of that came into play forcefully as Amy sang. After that we dated again, and something very precious began to develop between us. I was praying, "Lord, please make clear to me your direction. With my emotional approach toward life, with all of my sentimentality, I do not want to make an emotional decision. I want to know that I am led of God in this vital decision." And I prayed that way all summer. When we saw each other again in the fall after a separation, all that we had known had grown and deepened and strengthened. I came to a great awareness that it was God's purpose for me to marry this woman. I knew that I loved her and that I wanted that love to grow in depth and maturity and to be permanent. So I spoke with her and asked her to marry me. And she said, "Yes, I will." And so, on Valentine's Day 1973, we were married.

It has been more than fifteen years now, and we have had our adjustments, our ups and downs, our challenges. But we have always had a deep commitment to Jesus Christ to love each other and to make our marriage work. I have never been unfaithful to Amy; I have never betrayed her loyalty; she has never betrayed mine. Our marriage is stronger, better, and more productive now than it ever has been. We have one seven-year-old daughter, and, of course, have great love for her. She has been such an exciting fulfillment of our connection with each other. We are not overly sentimental about the challenges of marriage in this latter part of the twentieth century, but we know that God's biblical principles do work. And our excitement about that knows no boundaries.

God built you to be completed by your relationships with others. You desire intimacy, companionship, friendship. But in order to have quality relationships you must resolve an inner battle: your greatest desires are fulfilled in relationships; yet your greatest fears are of those same relationships. You want intimate relationships but fear them at the same time because of the potential for the damaging, destructive feeling of personal rejection. There is no greater blow to the ego. You want to look someone in the eye and care about him and have him care about you, yet you have this tremendous fear swirling around waiting to clutch at your throat.

One five-year study stated that the number-one cause of failure is lack of social skill—being unable to have good relationships with other people [Carole Hyatt and Linda Gottlieb, *When Smart People Fail* (Simon and Schuster, 1987)]. The Carnegie Institute also determined that 85 percent of all people who fail in their work lack social skills and do not have good relationships with other people.

Imagine you are at a theme park, and a bus of senior citizens pulls up. People in their seventies and eighties have gotten off the bus and are standing waiting for their tour guide to come. Can you see the two women who came together, the man with the walker, the woman with the cane? As you look at this group, can you see yourself? When you get to this point in your life, the only thing that will matter will be your relationships. Financial security will be important but your relationships will be more important. Do you want to be a disgruntled, bitter old woman who has driven her family away? Do you want to be a man whose children have grown up

21

not loving him or knowing him or even liking him? Picture yourself and determine where you will be in thirty, forty, fifty years *in your relationships.*

RUPTURING A RELATIONSHIP

What brings the strain into a relationship and ruptures it? Why is it that you can stand and look into someone's eyes in a wedding ceremony full of love, promise, excitement, and potential, feeling the thrill of that moment, and then begin to pull apart? Let's look at four things that will rupture your relationships.

1. Neglect. Neglect will cool the flame, pull you apart. Neglect will weaken the bond between you. Neglect is a failure to look, to listen, to touch, to feel, to share with another person. It is a terrible rejection to feel that someone is not listening to you. One of the first signs a psychologist looks for when counseling a couple is if they look into each other's eyes as they communicate. A test group of middle-class couples on the West Coast agreed to be wired up with microphones and meters for one year to see how many minutes they spent with their husbands or wives in quality communication. Out of 10,680 minutes in a week, the average length of time came to 17 minutes. This did not include talking about challenges or kids, but one-to-one, heart-to-heart contact with another human being. No wonder some people feel so lonely even in their marriages. No wonder they are frustrated. Home is empty; it is hollow.

2. Manipulation. There are two kinds of manipulation—passive and active. Passive manipulation means you pout or become very quiet, or you get sick. You do anything to manipulate another person to get him to do what you want. It shows disrespect to the other person. Active manipulation uses temper, anger, and hostility.

I believe the threat of embarrassment is one of the most serious uses of manipulation in the family today. I asked a young married couple I was counseling about the biggest hassle they had. They looked at each other and looked at me and said, "We're not trying to pick on anybody, but it's her mother. She always tries to maneuver us and squeeze us into a certain position." I asked how the mom did this, and the wife said, "She tries to embarrass us publicly, and she gives us a signal that it is coming. What can we do?" I told them to tell her they loved and respected her, but if she wanted to see them anymore, she must stop the manipulation.

You can do this in your business, in your family, in your friendships. If you are a manipulator, you will rupture your relationships.

3. Possessiveness. Do you know what's wrong with possessiveness? It is almost always disguised as concern. When you say, "Well, I only did it for your own good because I thought you wanted me to do it," you're possessing someone, controlling him—and trying to cover it up.

23

Something jolted me as I was going over the material for this book. I had my wife, Amy, read it, and she said to me, "Ron, this is one of your problems. Sometimes you smother me to death. I know you love me and want me with you all the time, but sometimes you are just too possessive."

Men frequently do this to women. A man's role is to be the head of his home, but it doesn't mean he should smother another person. And possessiveness will do that to a relationship.

4. *Overdependency.* A relationship is ruptured by overdependency. It is similar to possessiveness but somewhat different. Overdependency means you drain another person. You don't stand on your own two feet. You expect your husband or wife to meet every need you will ever have. Let me ask you an honest question. As you have grown up and become an adult, what kind of friends do you usually drop? The ones that control and smother. Then why in the world would you want to let that kind of immaturity control your marriage?

RUINING A RELATIONSHIP

You can rupture a relationship without ruining it. Now I want to show you three ways to ruin a relationship.

1. *Frozen anger.* If you have anger somewhere in your past, it will freeze the relationship. Frozen anger is never dealt with; it is always there.

I know people who are ripped to pieces on the inside because they have all of this anger and resentment and have never dealt with it. If you have a sweet Christian face masking a turmoil of bitterness and resentment, you have got to get help from a counselor or pastor.

2. *Punishment.* A determination to punish the other person will ruin a relationship. You would not believe the number of wives and husbands I have counseled who admit to me that their real goal in life is revenge on their husbands or their wives or their children. They want to punish them—not help them, not build them, not recover them—but punish them. They want to see them hurt, to see them suffer. Of course, they may not say this in so many words because it wouldn't sound right; but it is nevertheless true.

I counseled one mother who was so mad at her daughter and son-in-law that she took it out on their children, her own grandchildren. She even had prayed for God to bring vengeance on them just because they would not do what she wanted. Do you see what can happen to human beings?

3. *Betrayal.* Betrayal in a marriage is a choice to shift your affections to someone else. You're not just swept along by passion. You're not just controlled by sexual energy. You make a choice to betray someone. You make a choice to betray your vows and your family. You choose to unbond with someone to whom you have been bonded. You choose betrayal.

I want to share something very personal with you. Proverbs 5:3-5 is a passage that talks about a man going to a woman's house for a sexual encounter. It says, "Her feet go down to death; her steps lead straight to the grave" (NIV). Do you know what happens when you choose to sexually connect with another man or another woman to whom you are not married? After you have had a sexual encounter, life as you have known it will cease to exist. It's that serious. It is a spiritual matter before God. There will be something deeply ruptured within you as a human being, something horribly changed. You are dealing with God's laws here. They always operate; they always work. You prosper when you obey them; you are destroyed when you break them. Don't let Satan trick you into betraying your marriage.

RECOVERING A RELATIONSHIP

I have really good news. If you have already messed up, remember that no failure is permanent. You can be recovered! Here are the principles of recovery of a relationship.

1. *Forgiveness.* Do you know why you probably don't like the word *forgiveness?* Because you think it implies giving up and letting your spouse get away with something. But forgiveness is not tolerance and leniency. True forgiveness will release tremendous freedom in your life. If you don't forgive, you're the one who

suffers and lives with it day and night. It will hold you a slave for life, and you will pay the price emotionally. Many cases of mental illness with which psychologists deal are caused when lack of forgiveness of something in the person's past poisons him.

At some point forgiveness is a decision you must make. There's a humorous story in Lewis Carroll's *Through the Looking Glass.* At one point the queen and king are talking. The king says, "The horror of that moment, I shall never forget." "You shall forget," the queen replies, "that is, if you don't make a memorandum out of it." You may need to use some mental discipline to make yourself stop repeating over and over the thing that hurt you. Sometimes you may have to love a person and forgive him but tell him that unless he straightens up, you cannot work with him.

Some of you have been really hurt and don't know how to forgive. That's where God can help you because the power of forgiveness comes through knowing Jesus Christ. He can help you forgive things you never thought were possible to forgive. If you don't have the power to forgive, turn to Jesus Christ.

2. *Rebonding.* You must learn the principle of rebonding that which has broken. How do you do it? Bonding refers to the way concrete slowly sets. You need to set a relationship so that it will have permanence. If you are weak anywhere in your marriage, isn't it because you have not

been bonding to each other and not doing the things that create the bond? I read about one man's concept of each of us having a love bank where others make deposits and withdrawals. If you make too many withdrawals from somebody else's love bank, that person will stop feeling love for you. You need to make deposits into his love bank by doing loving things—bonding. How do you really rebond something that is broken?

There are four Greek words that describe different kinds of love—*eros, phileo, storge,* and *agape.* They work together to form a good marriage.

Eros describes physical, sexual love. You must have the passion, the magic, the fire, the spark, the excitement.

Phileo is the word for friendship, comradeship. It describes shared interests and activities.

Storge describes nurturing—the word the Greeks use for being a good mom and dad. You should parent your husband, your wife.

Agape means a commitment to love each other. It is a targeted affection. It is a choice to love no matter what.

You rebond and rebuild the above kinds of love; you do whatever it takes to build trust.

3. Get rid of false pride and sophistication. Don't lose the ability to be free and spontaneous with each other. Act like a child. A child will come to you, love you, and hug you, and is not embarrassed to say, "I love you." A husband especially may need to learn to be childlike and express love to his wife. Show her love and affection. I have a friend in Lexington, Kentucky, whom I visit every couple of months. He owns a multimillion-dollar thoroughbred horse farm. His house has twenty-eight thousand square feet. He is so down to earth and loving and tender, and he doesn't have false pride, ego, and sophistication. He just cares about people, and so can you.

4. *Share a dream together.* Work together, build together. It will help to rebond your relationship.

This phrase will sum up everything I have said: You must nourish and cherish or you will perish. Doesn't this apply to your marriage, to your business, to your friends?

Quality relationships are the building blocks of all success. Even financial achievement is bitter and empty without someone with which to enjoy it. There is no ultimate fulfillment in isolation. You are defined by your relationships to other people and to God. I urge you, for the sake of your own future as well as those for whom you care, to take an honest relationship journey. Your final goal: a healthy, happy, well-adjusted, productive life, centered in Jesus Christ and in right relationships with other people.

TWO
COMMITMENT TO COMMUNICATION

Communication skills in your marriage are crucial. How you communicate with your husband or wife forms the basis of how you communicate with other people. So take a close look at your marriage. Some men can be pretty stubborn, and if there's a problem in the marriage, they have difficulty admitting it. But they are not communicating and they know it. And many wives feel frustrated with the communication in their marriages. They can talk with their husbands about a lot of different subjects but don't seem able to penetrate to deep levels in heart communication.

When I began to date Amy, my emotions were powerfully affected. I remember going into the college cafeteria and ordering something. They gave me a plate of Jell-O, which wasn't what I wanted. But I was so entranced with Amy that I didn't even realize I was eating something else.

It was amazing. I went in day after day and ordered Jell-O—it was all I could think to order.

Look back to the early years of your courtship and marriage. In those early stages of romance, you found each other fascinating. You were beginning to explore the other individual—what he likes, where she goes, what is his favorite food, what is her favorite perfume. You were hooked, and all you could think about was the other person. And you seemed to have no trouble communicating. The reason was because of your mutual fascination with each other.

As you got into the marriage you found that there were all kinds of frictions, adjustments, ups, and downs. Suddenly communication was not as easy as it had been. Before you were married, you didn't share all the problems in your lives. You shared the good times. You had fun together. You were living an illusion. The day-to-day challenges of life that force you to communicate weren't there.

Now that you are married, you have work, home, adjustments, and maybe children—a whole different set of challenges. They will test your commitment, your seriousness, your walk with God. Those of you who make it will have a wonderful, fulfilling, tremendous marriage. But you must learn to communicate.

Your marriage should be the most intimate, enjoyable, fulfilling relationship in your life. But what if it's not that wonderful, not that fulfilling? You have to pay a price to get it there. If you live your life without that kind of closeness, fulfillment, and excitement with another man or another woman, then you will miss something God intended in your marriage. You will be forever unfulfilled.

BARRIERS TO COMMUNICATION

In a marriage, the basic sense of who you are can be tested beyond anything you ever dreamed. Because of the intimacy of the relationship, you open yourself up to your spouse in a way no one else ever sees you. But this can set you up to fear rejection from this person who knows you so well. Rejection in a marriage is horrible. Sexual rejection is particularly difficult to take. For a man, it is one of the most brutal forms of emotional isolation and makes him feel less than a man. And sexual rejection makes a woman feel like less of a woman. Because of this ego sensitivity, communication in marriage is not easy. You may not speak with each other in a straightforward, totally honest way in order to protect yourself. And the more you protect yourself, the less intimacy you have. Intimacy depends on closeness and trust. You have to be willing to risk your ego and risk rejection or else you will never come to the fully intimate, wonderful, incredible closeness that God created you to have in the privacy of the marriage relationship. And you will never communicate very well. Let's look at several specific barriers to intimate communication.

Different Backgrounds

You will have some radical differences in background with your mate, even if you grew up next door to each other. You have had a whole different set of family memories and experiences. It doesn't mean that one set of experiences is right and the other is wrong. They are just different.

One difference between my background and Amy's involves food. My mom grew up on a farm and fixed enormous meals. For breakfast she prepared pork chops, fried chicken, bacon, biscuits, milk gravy, sausage, fried apples, fried potatoes, and eggs. That was a pretty standard breakfast.

Amy grew up in a very different home. It was every man for himself. There may be some sweet rolls or donuts and milk and juice in the refrigerator. When we got married, Amy didn't get up three hours early and fix me a feast for breakfast. I felt hurt. We had to talk about it. We had some big differences in our backgrounds that made us hurt each other unintentionally. These things may sound silly and dumb, but if you get enough differences in your backgrounds they can become real problems if you don't deal with them. You need to have the courtesy to respect your mate's background, acknowledging that it is not *wrong,* just different.

Different Temperaments

I have heard people say that opposites attract. But I'm not sure that's accurate. Opposites are interesting, but the more opposite you are in marriage, the harder it can be to have closeness in your relationship. For instance, if you are a real talker and he is the strong, silent type, it may work out well in your dating. But when you get into the marriage and he never talks to you, it will drive you crazy.

I counseled a woman who said, "I married a man who was so different from me because I thought he could provide me some security. I married a man I normally don't even like." She was an artist and very flighty; he was an accountant, the solid-like-a-rock type. She said his dullness began to drive her to tears, and they had only been married a few years. What she formerly looked at as strength and stability, she began to see as boredom and dullness.

If you are like this couple, you can develop a wonderful relationship. But you have to realize that differences in temperament are a challenge to be overcome.

Amy and I are alike in many ways. But there is one big difference between us: we relax differently. When Amy relaxes, she gets very quiet, quite different from her usual behavior. She can go an hour and say nothing. The more I relax, however, the louder and harder I talk. For the first two or three years we were married, I was baffled because I thought something was wrong when Amy became quiet. It took me a long time to accept that that was her way of relaxing.

Different Needs

Much of the adjustment in marriage happens when certain needs aren't being met. A woman grows up watching her father play certain roles, and she expects similar things from her husband. She may try to force her husband to be like her dad. Or a man may try to force his wife to be like his mother. This is not fair. You need to look at the person and see him or her as someone you love, respect, and value. Try to understand his or her background and temperament.

A real turning point in this area came for Amy and me in our early years when I was still in graduate school. There was something really wrong with us emotionally that day. We were conflicting in a serious way. I could not understand why Amy had taken a certain position. She was being so stubborn. As I was walking out the door of our apartment, I turned and walked back in and sat Amy down on the floor with me. I looked her right in the face and said, "Listen, I don't understand why you said what you said. I feel hurt." And she said, very strongly, "Well, I don't understand what you said and I feel hurt."

We talked for two hours nonstop. My number one objective was to understand her, not force her to accept my position. All of a sudden, it was as if a light clicked on in my brain, and I said, "Oh, you feel this way because your mom and your dad operated like this when you were growing up!" She said, "That's right. That's why I feel this way." And the reason I felt the way I did was because that was the way my dad handled similar situations. We began to laugh and fell into each other's arms. The whole thing was just a great relationship builder for us. We didn't give up or let our background differences create a barrier to our communication and a barrier to our intimacy.

DIFFERENCES BETWEEN THE SEXES

Next I want to look at the differences between men and women and their specific needs, which can become barriers to communication.

Men

The key to understanding a man and being able to communicate with him is to understand his ego needs. Dr. Willard F. Harley, Jr., a Christian psychologist in the Midwest, writes in *His Needs, Her Needs* (Revell, 1986): "A man's primary needs come in five areas: sexual fulfillment, recreational companionship, an attractive wife, domestic support, and admiration and respect." Let's take a look at these.

1. Admiration and respect. God has made men in such a way that they have tremendous need, not just desire, for admiration and respect. It is a primary need for a man, and not something he can do without and still be wholly a man. And if you are going to communicate with a man, you must keep this in mind. The apostle Paul, an early Christian writer, speaks of a woman's need to give great respect and support to her husband in Ephesians 5:33. This may surprise some women because they have been conditioned to think of men as strong and tough, but a man's ego is really fragile. When he experiences challenges or tries to cope with failure in his life, he needs to come home to a wife who builds him up with great doses of respect and admiration. More important than any need in my life is for Amy to respect me. That's one reason I work hard and try to build our future both spiritually and financially.

The other side of the coin is that the man should love his wife in such a way that he earns her respect and admiration. He can't demand that she respect him. If he does this like a tyrant, he will succeed in choking her emotionally and keep her from loving him and respecting him. Men need to create an atmosphere where their families will admire their work and leadership.

2. Sexual fulfillment. A man also has great sexual needs, and there is nothing wrong with this. If you grew up in a home where sex was seen as dirty and unclean, then you received an unbiblical, ungodly view of sex. According to the Bible, sex is good. Proverbs 5:18-19 says, "Be happy, yes, rejoice in the wife of your youth. Let her breasts and tender embrace satisfy you. Let her love alone fill you with delight." In the original Hebrew text of those verses, the words are sexually graphic, X-rated. They are words that have to do with a woman's sexual responsiveness.

I remember a doctor in his eighties who told me that he loved sex at least two or three times a week, and looked forward to it; it kept him young. A man has great sexual tension, need, and desire. God's perfect intention is for husband and wife to communicate sexually and emotionally in such a beautiful way that all of it blends together. Problems come because men and women are so different sexually, and they don't communicate their needs.

3. Recreational companionship. Men are famous for their tendency to "pal around" with other men. Most men never stop looking for fun things to do. A man's commitment to his marriage is deepened when this need for fun is consistently met within the marriage. Amy and I make a list weekly of recreational activities we'd like to do. We may not like each item the other selects but our goal is to list enough fun opportunities that we will find something enjoyable we can do together. This has enriched us for years, and we have satisfaction in our companionship.

4. An attractive wife. Visual stimulation is a major factor of male sexuality. Men are greatly affected by what they see. My purpose is not to load you with guilt if you consider yourself unattractive, but it will strengthen your relationship if you make your appearance a priority.

This is not to say you become a "sex object"; rather you exercise wisdom in looking your best. You'll be thankful for the results in your marriage.

5. Domestic support. A wife's loyalty and love is vital to a man's mental stability and emotional welfare. Men often battle immense pressure in business affairs. Their egos are damaged through the constant infighting in modern corporate life. A man's work performance is a critical expression of his personality, even involving his sexuality. A wife is a rock of support in a very stormy sea. He may not always admit his need for you, his wife, but the need is decidedly there. When you are his most loyal friend you will add immeasurably to the success of your husband and the success of your marriage.

Women

The key word to understanding women is emotion. Emotion is not a weak word. It does not mean that women are illogical; it is not a statement of inferiority. But women do operate differently than men. A woman has a tremendous need emotionally for intimate, undivided attention from her husband. She has a great need of protection and security. She needs deep communication and understanding.

1. Affection. Harley says that one need for a woman is affection. Affection can be hugging, touching, kissing, and holding hands, without necessarily leading to sex. I will admit that even to this day, after fifteen years of marriage, if my wife even brushes my hand gently during the day, I automatically think of sex. But she may be wanting just a moment of soft touch and closeness, and that's extremely valuable to her. A husband needs to develop greater skills in the area of affection if he wants to communicate to the precious individual whom God has allowed him to marry.

2. *Conversation.* A woman also needs conversation. When you come home, she wants to know every little detail of what you have done all day. And she wants to tell you about her day. Will you love her enough to meet this need?

I often find it difficult to tell Amy the details of my day. I have usually spoken more than once to large groups and counseled dozens of people. The last thing I want is to relive all those conversations. But this is so vital to Amy's sense of closeness to me that I have disciplined myself to tell her everything when I get home. I don't always feel like it; I do it because I love her.

3. *Honesty and openness.* If you manipulate her and she cannot trust you, then you begin to erode your intimate foundation and you begin to throw sexual fulfillment on the trash heap of your life. She has to know she can depend on what you tell her.

4. *Financial support.* That's security and protection, which we mentioned previously.

5. *Family commitment.* She needs to realize that you as a husband are going to provide a se-

41

cure home; you are committed to her and your children for the long term. You will not let go of your commitment to her.

Now what have we got? A man needing sexual fulfillment, recreational companionship, an attractive wife, domestic support in his home, and admiration and respect, and a woman whose great needs are for affection, conversation, honesty and openness, financial security, and family commitment. If one cannot understand where the other is coming from, you may never have the kind of intimacy that God can make available in your home.

Do you realize how important your sexual personalities are? Harley says the reason so many men and women fail to communicate with each other is simply because they don't understand the other's sexual and personal needs, and they don't respect those needs. If a man does not meet the emotional needs of his wife, she will not meet his sexual needs. It is automatic. Affection is the environment or the climate of the marriage while sex is a special event in that marriage. But you must have the environment of affection, warmth, and closeness before you can have the enjoyability of the special event. A man must understand that he is communicating something very negative to his wife if he has not been very loving and kind and then wants to jump into bed with her. She thinks he sees her as a sexual toy and nothing more, so she is offended and unresponsive. The husband then thinks his wife doesn't love him because she is not sexually responsive. If you don't communicate with each other, barriers go up, and you get into big trouble.

Do you want intimacy in your marriage? Do you want a life that for thirty, forty, or fifty years can create awesome fulfillment and satisfaction? Then you have to understand each other. Now I believe that no marriage can be totally fulfilled without building on the foundation of Jesus Christ. I don't say that to be offensive to you, but I say it because I believe it intensely and passionately. Beyond that, I believe the second foundation of your marriage is this commitment to communicate, this commitment to know each other. In the Bible, the word for "sexual union" is translated "to know." It is the deep, intimate blending of two personalities—far beyond biological connection—two people beginning to understand each other, to love each other. And it is the most beautiful experience in human life apart from knowing God.

My good friend Dexter Yager is a committed Christian and a very successful businessman. One of the things that most impresses me about him is that he is a man of great strength and courage who has made an effort over the years to love and understand his wife both emotionally and sexually. She is in love with him, and he is in love with her. Communication and commitment are most important to understanding the differences between the sexes.

BUSY SIGNALS

Have you ever found yourself trying to communicate but getting a busy signal? Let's now look at several different types.

1. Hearing without listening. You are physically hearing sounds but not really listening to what the person is saying. You may already have your mind made up, and you're just waiting for the speaker to shut up so you can say what you want to say. This is not communication. It's not even respecting another person. Can you think of anything more insulting to a wife than for a husband to continually appear to be listening but never hear her? What frustration and disappointment! You can't operate like that if you want the deepest, most intimate marriage you can have.

You can accomplish more in a conversation by listening well to a person than you can by talking to him or her. Try this the next opportunity you have: let the other person do most of the talking, and he will go away saying what a great conversation he had with you because you listened to him and valued him.

2. Not looking each other in the eye. I once observed a couple in a restaurant talking to each other. They kept trying to communicate, but something was not right. I could not put my finger on it for awhile, but it finally came to me: they would not look each other in the eye while they were talking.

One very important thing I learned from the president of the college I attended was how to really connect emotionally with a person with whom you were having a conversation. When he talked to me, he wouldn't look at anybody else. He gave me his undivided attention, and I felt great. Even when other people would walk by and say hello, he would not respond to them but kept looking me right in the eye.

Do you look at your mate when you are talking, or do you do a thousand other things and never really communicate through your eyes that you really care, that you're listening, that you understand?

3. *Too busy to talk.* Another way to give a busy signal is to be too busy. I am shocked at the number of couples who tell me it has been so long since they have been alone with each other—out to dinner or a night away. You must take the time. Don't say how important your marriage is if you don't give it time.

4. *Struggling for power.* When you have power struggles in your home and are always trying to jockey for position you are sending a serious busy signal. Don't try to dominate your husband or wife; love him, understand her, know him. If you are always in these power struggles, it will shatter your communication, destroy your intimacy, and can even wipe out your marriage.

SERIOUS BARRIERS

Let's turn to some more serious barriers to communication.

1. Neurotic needs. These are normal needs that become abnormal because they have been unmet for so long. A person needs sexual fulfillment, but if it becomes obsessive or possessive, and he resorts to abuse to get what he wants, then it is neurotic. A wife needs security and protection, but if she won't allow her husband to take any risks, the situation has become extreme. A husband needs admiration from his wife, but if he becomes insanely jealous whenever she speaks to another man and imagines all sorts of sordid things going on, his need is no longer within healthy boundaries.

A neurotic need is almost always rooted in a person's childhood. One woman described to me the needs she had had in her first marriage, which ended in divorce. Then she told me of all the needs she had in her second marriage, and it was in trouble. So I asked her about her mom and dad. She said, "Oh, they were divorced when I was a child." As we talked we discovered that she was operating on the basis of a tremendous need for security and closeness that had been created early in her life because of her mom and dad's divorce. She was putting a lot of pressure on her husband, was often depressed, full of anxiety, and living with the fear of losing her own marriage. This climate made her relationship difficult to handle, and it was creating strain. If you suspect neurotic needs are playing a role in your marriage, you may need to find a good marriage counselor to help you work through the problems.

Some neurotic needs are less complex and do not require professional counseling. You just need to get alone with your spouse and pour out your heart to him or her. Tell him what you are feeling—jealousy, fear, depression, sexual compulsiveness. This will strengthen your relationship as you become vulnerable, opening your heart and admitting your need for your spouse's help.

2. *Unrealistic expectations.* If your expectations are gigantically high when you come into a marriage, they will automatically become barriers to communication. You may expect your husband to be just like your father or expect your wife to be just like your mother. When your expectations are not met, you become disappointed and you pout. A woman may suffer from the Cinderella complex, expecting Prince Charming to sweep her off her feet and carry her off to a wonderful castle. A man may have unrealistic sexual expectations, thinking he will live in a sexual paradise for the rest of his life and that it will be absolutely awesome, incredible, and wonderful all the time. If these things don't hold true, disappointment will follow, bringing serious barriers to communication.

Remember this: your expectations are almost always founded in your selfishness. You selfishly expect your mate to meet your desires. But marriage takes work, work, work. You must think of what you have to do to make it work.

Years ago, I was counseling a high-school

couple, and they came to me very agitated at each other. The problem really wasn't all that serious, but I remember how she looked. She said, "I just know I love him." I asked her how she knew. She replied, "Because when I'm with him, he makes me so happy." Later I talked to him, and he said something very similar, "Ron, when I'm with her, she makes me feel so good."

Do you see how self-centered those statements are? I love her because *she* makes *me* so happy. There is no concentration on the other person's needs or how to build up him or her. It is all self-centered. The more self-centered your relationship, the more unrealistic your expectations tend to be. You fail to realize that fulfillment in your marriage will come to the degree to which you contribute.

3. *"Shoulditis."* "Shoulditis" is closely related to expectations. Instead of communicating, you are always thinking of what the other person *should* do. "He should understand." "She should have sex with me more." The danger point is when you start thinking of the other person as being unfair to you. Selfishness is at work again. And if your marriage is worth what you say it's worth, you'll want to drop all of this "should" stuff, unfair stuff, and learn to reach your spouse's heart. That may be tough for you. And that's the reason I urge you repeatedly to turn to Jesus Christ and let him give you the power to love with the capacity you've never dreamed could exist in your spiritual life. You need his

help, and your marriage needs his help.

4. *"Neveritis."* You overstate and exaggerate everything. "He never helps me." "She never goes with me where I want to go." The moment you overstate it, you give the other person an excuse to get out of it because he thinks, "I did help her last Thursday, Friday, and Saturday." She might say, "Yes, I do go where you want to go, just like a couple of weeks ago . . . ." He may not help enough. She may not do as much as you would like, but you are still overstating it. That's a barrier to communication both ways because you see the other person in a distorted way.

5. *Authoritarianism.* You have to be the boss no matter what. I'll tell you something straight: if a man is unfair to his wife, too hard on her, treats her like a child, and says he is doing it because he is the boss, that man is weak and insecure.

A man once said to me, "I believe the old proverb holds true for a wife as well as for children: 'A wife should be seen and not heard.'" A wife is not a child! God never intended that. A man is to be a leader, but a loving leader. And the wife is a created, valued partner. If you are the iron-fisted tyrant to your family, will you grow up and let God change you? Will you let him get rid of your feeling of inferiority, your fear that if you don't dominate your wife you are less than a man? People who cannot accept themselves and their limitations are people who are insecure and feel inferior. This can destroy intimacy, wreck communication, and absolutely devastate a marriage.

6. Spiritual resistance. This is a man or woman who resists God and will not grow. I'm talking about a marriage where one spouse does not know Christ and the other one does. If your husband does not know Jesus Christ, you are making a terrible mistake if you try to pressure him to come to God. He will reject God, thinking he will prove his manhood by rejecting your pressure, and he will become very, very stubborn. If a man is spiritually resistant, you have to love him and pray for him. And the same goes for a woman.

Let me say something to those of you who are not right with God. If your wife or husband knows the living, loving God through Christ and you don't, there will always be a level of intimacy you will never know until you can share with him or her spiritually in the love of Jesus Christ. You are missing the greatest dimension of your life. Why miss it any longer?

BUILDING BLOCKS

In order to build a right relationship from which communication can flow naturally, you need to learn to handle differences in a positive way. You need to learn how to stay friends when you fight. Here are several tips on this.

1. Avoid primitive weapons. A woman should not use her great powers of emotion to attack her husband. If a wife resorts to crying or becomes cold and emotionally distant to punish him, that is a primitive weapon. It's not worthy of her. A man should never resort to using his physical strength as a weapon. If a husband ever lays a hand on his wife, it's primitive and disgusting. It's a way of trying to pound her into submission, forcing her to listen. A wife doesn't have to put up with that. Using sex is another primitive weapon and can be used by both men and women. Any of these weapons put up barriers to communication. They only create problems; they never solve conflicts.

I read an article recently written by a daughter about her parents' forty years of marriage. In it she described her mom and dad as having deep differences that were never settled. The mother would withdraw sex from the father as punishment. He would get angry and lose his temper, breaking and smashing things. Now, after forty years, when the differences come up, he just leaves the house for hours at a time. They never sleep together. They never communicate. The daughter described it as horrible, and said, "I never want that in my marriage."

You may think you are getting a victory by crying, smashing things, or withholding sex. But all you are doing is creating resentment and bitterness that someday will kill your love and even the love of your children. So, please avoid the use of primitive weapons to punish your mate.

2. *Never use ridicule or mockery.* This is show-

ing terrible disrespect to a person. You can disagree furiously, but don't ever do it in a cutting, sarcastic way.

3. Bury past experiences. Don't ever pull up a past experience or event and beat your spouse over the head with it. You are just avoiding the current situation, and you'll never settle your differences that way. Some things may never be truly settled, but at least you can learn to compromise enough to resolve the past event and keep it in the past.

4. Accept changes. Remember that everyone is changing. Give your spouse room to grow. What worked in communication three years ago may not work today. Accept the fact that he or she is changing, because if a person isn't changing, he is dying. A successful marriage is one that continues to adapt to change.

5. Always show respect. Confide in a way that you remain friends. The one person to whom you never want to show disrespect is the woman you love, the husband you live with.

6. Be willing to compromise. You don't have to be right all of the time. Don't live as the disgusting "know-it-all." Be able to say, "I see that we have different ideas. We're even mad about this." But don't say, "You're wrong." Be willing to give. "Let's see how we arrived at these problems and how we can compromise."

7. Speak positively. Always look for fresh new ways to say three things: I love you, I appreciate you, and I respect you.

8. Never attack. What happens when you attack? You create one of two responses: the other person either withdraws in defense or fights back. Both types of response kill communication. Remember, you are not trying to win an argument or prove a position or out-debate your spouse. You're trying to love him or her. You are building a relationship, a love, a life.

9. Keep to the issue. Don't get off on personalities; stay on the issue. Don't attack your spouse with personal remarks.

10. Remember that you love him or her. This is most important!

Remember also that God loves you. He wants to help your marriage, and you need his help. Communicate and work out your problems, and in fifty or sixty years you will be happy because you will have built the most precious and priceless thing in human experience apart from God—a real marriage, a true friendship, and a great love. No amount of money in the world can pay for what that's worth.

THREE
DANGER SIGNALS IN MARRIAGE

I was visiting a friend of mine in Kentucky recently, and I spent about an hour with her praying over things. She is a very wonderful, godly woman and a great counselor to me. As we talked, she said to me, "Ron, the thing that has impressed me over the years has been your commitment to your marriage. You have always worked unreservedly to build the kind of relationship that God can honor and can use." I took that as a very meaningful compliment but also as a tremendous challenge to continue working on the quality of our relationship. Amy and I have been married fifteen years now, and I would like to share with you three ingredients I have found essential to a good marriage.

1. Uncommon dream. In the first two or three years we were married God began to develop within me an uncommon dream for an uncommon marriage. We had had the privilege of going through some outstanding marriage counseling with a godly man by the name of David Seamands. He was our pastor at school and he married us. Dr. Seamands warned us repeatedly not to have unrealistic expectations, not to go into marriage expecting perfection or smooth sailing all the way. We were to go into marriage with realism, with our feet on the ground. Yet having unrealistic expectations is not the same as having high expectations. Unrealistic expectations will bring you crashing in terrible flames to the ground. But an uncommon dream is what God has given me with Amy. I do not want anything mediocre about my marriage. I do not want anything common or ordinary. I want an uncommon dream to unfold through our years together.

2. *Uncommon commitment.* In order to have an uncommon dream, you need to have uncommon commitment or it will not work. In Matthew 19:5, Jesus quoted a verse found in Genesis 2:24: "A man shall leave his father and mother, and shall cleave to his wife; and the two shall become one flesh" (NASB). The word *cleave* is a key term here that literally means "bonded together," bonded as if glued together. Complete unity. It is that type of unity and commitment that builds an uncommon dream.

Many of you have priorities with your employment or with your children. You have dreams of what you want to accomplish in life. But I want to challenge you to develop uncommon dreams for your marriage relationships. Have an un-common dream and an uncommon commitment that will keep you straight regardless of pressures to pull you off course. Everything hangs on the uncommon commitment.

3. *Uncommon friendship.* The last thing you need to develop is an uncommon friendship. Amy asked me recently what was the one thing I hoped for when we first married. After thinking for a moment, I said, "The one thing I wanted was the deepest, richest, most precious, intimate, fulfilling friendship imaginable. I wanted to be the closest friend in the world to you and you to be the closest friend in the world to me." That is exactly what Genesis 2 talks about. At that dramatic moment when God brings Eve to Adam, he is thoroughly overwhelmed. He cannot believe his eyes. He realizes that here is his completion, the woman fit for him. The expression "bone of my bone, flesh of my flesh" expresses this depth of friendship. And that was my goal—an uncommon friendship.

I believe God wants you to have an uncommon dream, an uncommon commitment, and an uncommon friendship. I will do anything, pay any price, God being my witness, to have the uncommon dream with my wife, to have an uncommon commitment to her to make it work, and to have that uncommon friendship with her. And for more than fifteen years it has been coming true. It is not easy. There are many ups and downs but that uncommon dream is worth grasping with everything you have and every ounce of energy God can give you.

SIX DANGER SIGNALS IN MARRIAGE

During our tenth year of marriage, Amy and I realized we were on shaky ground. We weren't in desperate trouble, nothing was really urgent, but for some reason that tenth year of marriage was very dangerous. We could sense it and feel it before we could express it.

We sat down one evening and talked and prayed for about two hours about the need to become alert to what was happening. There were very subtle warning lights going off to both of us. We did not know quite how to handle it at first since we had been close for some years and had developed intimacy with each other. But there were these danger signals, and we realized that if we did not come to grips with them and handle them properly, we could be in serious trouble.

1. Discontent. The first serious danger signal is a feeling of discontent—very subtle, slow, almost unnoticeable, but there it is. My wife and I had begun to feel discontent.

Discontent is fed by continually comparing your husband or wife with someone else—his sexuality and talents, her abilities or success. You are always holding your partner up to careful scrutiny, and you are looking at him, trying to find a flaw, trying to pinpoint a problem.

I spoke a few years ago at a local church in Florida. There I spent some time talking to a woman who was greatly concerned about her husband's spiritual condition. He did not know Jesus Christ personally, and she prayed for him. Yet, she also hounded him, pressured him, and constantly held him up to personal scrutiny. She told him how he was failing spiritually. From a very sincere motivation, she was trying to make him conform to a Christian image. He came to one of our services, and seemed to care deeply for his wife. He was very generous in his compliments to her. Yet even in front of him she could not restrain herself from comparing him with the Christian men of the congregation. The discontent was beginning to develop.

Discontent is very self-centered. You are continually pushing your partner to be something you want him or her to be. And discontent is famous for complaining, always finding fault.

What is your basic attitude right now toward your husband or wife? Is there a feeling of discontent? Be totally honest. Are you beginning to feel that maybe life has dealt you a low blow? Why do you have to live with this cantankerous man? Why do you have to live with this uncooperative woman?

The positive and exciting news about danger signals is that they can serve as spark plugs to fixing the problem. So how do you handle discontent? Begin by thanking God for the person with whom you live. Thank God for his or her strengths. Thank God for his or her encouragement. It may not be easy at first, but do learn to thank God for this person. It is extremely difficult to thank God for someone and complain about him or her at the same time. The apostle Paul said in Philippians 4:11, "I have learned to be content whatever the circumstances" (NIV). In 1 Timothy 6:6, Paul wrote, "Godliness with contentment is great gain" (NIV). The psalmist wrote in Psalm 103:2, "Praise the Lord, O my soul, and forget not all his benefits" (NIV). Thank God for your spouse.

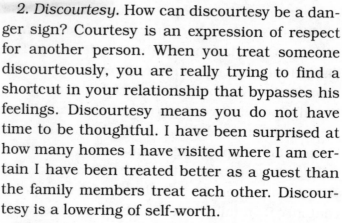

2. Discourtesy. How can discourtesy be a danger sign? Courtesy is an expression of respect for another person. When you treat someone discourteously, you are really trying to find a shortcut in your relationship that bypasses his feelings. Discourtesy means you do not have time to be thoughtful. I have been surprised at how many homes I have visited where I am certain I have been treated better as a guest than the family members treat each other. Discourtesy is a lowering of self-worth.

What do you do about discourtesy? I just bought a new riding lawn mower, and I read in the instructions that oil is crucial to adequately maintain the engine. Likewise it is the oil of courtesy that makes the machinery of marriage run smoothly. The Word of God actually says to be courteous in 1 Peter 3:8. Galatians 5:22 lists kindness as being a result of holy, spirit-filled living. Kindness is love in action. It is crucial to your marriage.

3. Destructive speech. I am talking about the kind of verbal attacks where you are critical, where you embarrass your partner, where you continually nag at him or her about something.

I was with a family just recently where the atmosphere was full of such strain I could hardly wait to leave. Perhaps you have heard the verse in Proverbs, "A constant dripping on a rainy day and a cranky [person] are much alike!" (TLB). I walked out of the house, looked at Amy, and said, "Drip, drip, drip." That was all we had heard, one little digging remark after another.

I was in a meeting with all of the churches in a community in Illinois a few years ago, and I went to dinner with a family, the husband being a key community leader and a strategic individual in setting up this crusade. They bowed their heads and the husband prayed. That was the last spiritual moment of the night. They dug at one another, cut one another, wounded one another. It was constant badgering, making jokes about one another. They did not do it bluntly but subtly using destructive speech.

Destructive speech shatters self-esteem. It may be your way for seeking revenge. If you are really trying to needle your partner about something, it may be that you have refused to forgive something in the past. Your destructive speech is the way you are venting your anger. Your resentment has built up, and it is coming out through destructive speech. Destructive speech erodes the foundation of your relationship. No one can take much without it having a danger-ous, negative effect. It builds resentment. Some-times you start throwing it back at the other person and it develops into a combat between you.

What is the opposite of destructive speech? Positive encouragement. The Bible says that a soft answer turns away anger (Proverbs 15:1). Psalm 15:3 says, "Anyone who refuses to slan-der others, does not listen to gossip, never harms his neighbor, . . . such a man shall stand firm forever" (TLB). The closest neighbor you have is the one with whom you live in marriage. Ephesians 4:30-31 says, "Let all bitterness, wrath, anger, clamor, and evil speaking be put away from you, with all malice. And be kind to one another, tenderhearted, forgiving one an-other, just as God in Christ also forgave you" (NKJV).

The most powerful element of that last verse is that the Bible actually tells you to put those things away. Do not do them any more. Just quit. Stop speaking with bitterness, anger, and wrath. Put it away from you and then forgive, be kind, express generosity with your speech.

I conducted a wedding several years ago at a church in Atlanta. It was a rather large wedding on a Saturday evening, and I will never forget part of the vows that couple took: "I will never publicly or privately embarrass you for any reason." A couple with that commitment is off to a good start.

4. *Deception.* You can call it deception. You can refer to it as plain dishonesty. Or you can say it is merely disguising the truth. All three statements really mean the same thing.

When I was speaking in Alabama last year, I walked through a large conference hall. There was a group of women in the corner, and they were discussing their husbands. Since they were talking rather loudly, I could not help but overhear their conversation. Two of the women were saying how they could get their husbands to do anything. They could manipulate the men and make them think it was their own idea. I could see them laughing and joking, and I was struck at the violation of the biblical principles of intimacy.

Do you know what manipulation really is? It is when you tell a half-truth, trick someone in a way, tell someone just enough of the truth to get his interest, draw him along just long enough to get him to do what you want. Manipulation is stealing another person's right of choice. You are stealing another person's right to choose his own reaction. You are an emotional thief.

What does deception do? Why is it a danger? It is an automatic barrier to intimacy. How can you have the closeness that God intends for you if there is constant manipulativeness, conniving, trying to get what you want?

I am not proud of it, but I have done this with my wife. For example, in the early years of our ministry, I did evangelistic crusades on weekends and in the summer. We traveled great distances and would get very tired driving. But I wanted to conserve money and drive straight through to our destination. I did not actually tell Amy this, however, and instead developed the great art of not accurately telling her how far we had to drive. I would look at a map, make a very generous estimate of the miles, and say, "Well, Amy, it looks like around three hundred miles." Amy would then say, "If it is really that close, we can do it. We don't have to stop." After we'd been driving awhile and it was getting late at night, we would see a sign for two hundred miles more. Needless to say, Amy was thoroughly disgusted and told me the truth of what was going on.

The whole point is that I manipulated the truth because I did not want to pay the money for a motel and I was afraid of Amy's response. I still struggle with this. Just a few months ago I did it again and God really convicted me of it. He's going to help me overcome this because I don't want to treat Amy with that kind of deceptiveness. She is too much of a treasure to me.

The opposite of deceptiveness is loving truthfulness. Some key verses are Psalm 15:2, 4: God commends the man or the woman "who speaks the truth from his heart, . . . who keeps his oath even when it hurts" (NIV). In other words, hold to the truth even if the truth hurts you. Another great verse God has really burned into my own heart is Psalm 51:6: "Surely you desire truth in the inner parts" (NIV). When you begin to manipulate and maneuver, replace it instantly with loving truthfulness.

One word of caution: I know some people who talk about speaking the truth in love. What they really mean, however, is they believe they have an excuse to hammer the daylights out of you. Don't misuse truth as another form of destructive speech.

5. *Dullness, boredom, routine.* Many people I talk to feel, in particular, romantic boredom. It seems strange to even put the words *romantic* and *boredom* together! But these people develop a routine and lose touch with each other.

Replace dullness with romantic excitement. Whenever you feel dullness coming, that ought to spur you to do something romantic whether or not you feel like it. Boredom is an indicator that you probably don't! Be careful of falling into the trap of thinking, *Maybe I've fallen out of love.* Once your eyes begin to roam, they will most likely find someone who can restore, temporarily and at great cost, the feelings of excitement. But love doesn't come and go like the tide; it's a commitment. Don't rely on the crest of emotion to carry you along. When you sense boredom and dullness creeping into your marriage, work to develop romantic excitement. Do something about it.

When was the last time you took her out to eat? or sent him a gift unannounced? Have you spent an evening alone together recently? There will always be pressures such as children, finances, or time. You have to want to fix the problem. You cannot have romantic excitement unless you do romantic things. The man often needs the most encouragement in this area and I suggest he take the lead. You must say no to a lot of competing areas and say yes to developing continual, romantic involvement with your wife, because dullness is a serious enemy, particularly in this generation of great sexual competition.

6. Distance. If the five previous signals go unheeded, distance will often develop between you. This is really the most serious danger signal of all: living in the same house but hardly knowing each other. So many people I have talked to have been together for years on top of years but really have no intimate involvement with each other.

Here are five characteristics of this danger signal of distance:

The first sign that distance is growing between you is if you are developing interests that pull you apart. Notice that I did not say developing other interests. My wife is an extremely talented, aggressive, energetic, capable person, and she thrives on activity. She loves challenging projects. She would be depressed if she didn't have something positive into which to pour her energies. I am glad for her to have these interests. But if we ever begin developing interests, activities, and hobbies that build a wedge between us, that is a danger signal, a sign of distance. I am not saying that you should not develop individual interests. Just don't ever let those interests pull you apart.

The second sign of distance is when you prefer other people's company. Be honest here. Do you prefer other people's company—male or female? Would you rather be with someone else most of the time?

The third sign is when you start putting your children ahead of your mate. God never intended that. God created marriage, obviously, before he created the reproduction of children. All through the Old Testament there are continual reminders of the building of a marital foundation. You choose each other; You bring children into the union. The greatest gift you can give your children is a healthy marriage. In that secure framework you can rear healthy children, and after those children are gone, you will still have each other. Of course, when a new baby enters the family, unusual demands are placed on the mother's time by necessity. But if this priority continues as the children grow older, distance will result. I'm convinced this is a harmful choice that undermines the partnership of the marriage. Placing your children ahead of your spouse creates distance.

Fourth is a slowing of growth together. In other words, are you growing in your Bible study together, in activities? Do you do things as a couple? You do not want one of you to grow at a certain rate and leave the other behind.

The fifth characteristic of distance is a weakening of sexual interest. I know that some people are more sexually responsive than others, and we will deal more with that later. But there is no such thing as a sexless marriage. Even in Scripture sex is a barometer of the marriage relationship, an indicator of closeness. A weakening of sexual responsiveness and interest toward your partner indicates that there is at least the beginning of emotional distance.

If you are having trouble with distance, let me give you four things to work on: (1) let God reveal and heal any bitterness, (2) tenderly touch each other more, (3) look each other in the eyes, and (4) express love to your spouse in his or her terms. I was in a marriage enrichment seminar a few years ago, and we were supposed to say to our spouses, "This is the way I show love to you." One man very proudly looked at his wife and said, "Why, I show love to you by doing . . . ," and he said a little thing he did. She looked at him in shock and said, "I was convinced all these years that you did that to irritate me. I hate it! I didn't say anything because I was trying to be loving toward you." So when I say to love someone in his terms, that is exactly what I mean. Learn how to express love in such a way that your spouse will appreciate it.

When you begin to feel distance, work on unity and oneness. Use these signs as spark plugs. Strive for what is put forth in Genesis 2:24: "For this cause a man shall leave his father and his mother, and shall cleave to his wife; and they shall become one flesh" (NASB). "One flesh" in the Bible means two things: sexual union and a deep, total blending of two personalities.

As you read this section on danger signals, I want you to look closely at your marriage. Discuss these signs with your spouse, talk about them, share your concerns, and pray together for God's healing in your marriage.

- Do you feel even a little discontent? Develop the art of gratitude.
- Are you having trouble with discourtesy? Learn to respond in ways of common decency.
- Are you guilty of destructive speech? Replace it with positive encouragement.
- Are you struggling with deceit or manipulativeness? Strive for honesty and loving truthfulness.
- What about dullness? Work together to find ideas that will generate romantic excitement.
- And how about distance? Ask God to give you unity, one flesh.

FOUR
SEXUAL SABOTAGE AND TEMPTATION

Some time ago my wife and I were conducting services at a family camp in Michigan. We became acquainted with a young, unmarried couple in leadership over the youth. They impressed us as having great spiritual and intellectual gifts, and all of the adults in the camp spoke highly of them and recommended them for spiritual leadership. About ten days into the camp, this couple asked if they could speak to us privately. We met them in a large outdoor tabernacle and they confessed to us tearfully the intense sexual struggles they were experiencing. They had been sleeping together for several years, and they told us a story of broken commitments and promises they had made to God. They had repented over and over and had asked for God's forgiveness but were repeatedly back in the same bondage in a matter of days. They had done everything they could to cover up their sin and had refused to tell anyone about it until that week when God's power became so real in their lives.

I was in a meeting dealing with businessmen in a mid-Louisiana community recently and found a similar reaction among some adult men who told me privately the great, severe battles with inner lust and sexual temptation.

In the course of another meeting with nearly one hundred men at a civic club, I mentioned a book dealing with overcoming the temptation of lust. Afterward, I was immediately surrounded by nearly twenty-five men. They were eager to find out more information on the book because of their difficulties in this area.

People everywhere are struggling with sexual temptations. My wife and I have counseled with dozens of couples in the last several years who have had varying degrees of difficulty in the area of understanding their sexuality. According to the Bible, there is a deep link between your sexuality and your personality. Leviticus 18 through 21 lists what is known as the Holiness Code of the Old Testament containing rules, regulations, and restrictions governing day-to-day practical affairs. And in this code God repeatedly gives important warnings about guarding your sexuality: Be careful because you are a sexual person. It is no surprise that Satan, the vicious, horrible enemy of your life, would attack you sexually. Knowing your weakness better than you, Satan attacks you in the form of sexual sabotage in order to wreck God's purpose for your life. Sabotage is attack from within, and Satan takes your normal desires and feelings, your passions and emotions, and twists them against yourself into a weapon dedicated to your destruction.

SATAN'S LIES

There are two lies Satan uses to sabotage your sexuality.

1. Sex is supreme in life. It is something that should dominate and control you, and you need to go after it with whatever it takes to have full and complete sexual fulfillment. What Satan does not want you to know, particularly if you are a teenager or single adult, is that his approach to sexuality is always self-centered and is inescapably controlled by your emotions.

A good friend of mine gave me permission to share his story. He is now a committed Christian and very active in our church in Atlanta. I'm going to call him Bill and his wife Linda. "A few years ago I was a sexual mess. I believed that my happiness in life was with different women. I slept for several months at a time with about eleven different women until I met Linda, and we lived together before we got married. It finally got to the point where sex was meaningless. It was like eating a box of chocolates: they were each a little different but essentially the same— it was all candy. Every woman started to be the same to me. Before we were married, Linda went to one party where she had sex with several different men in one night. She felt abused, used, and thrown away like rubbish.

"I want you to tell this story because last week a man at church told me that he has been a Christian for years. He grew up in a conservative Christian home and has never been unfaithful to his wife. But he feels as though he has missed something and is struggling with temptation. I looked at him and told him that the only thing he has missed is the wreckage. To this day I am haunted by all those women. My wife wakes up in the night struggling with her memories. We pray together that if there is any way for God to obliterate these memories, to please do it."

2. I have a right to meet my sexual needs. I have encountered Satan's second lie everywhere. People say, "I have a right to be sexually active, sexually free." But this is a distortion of the truth because you have no "right" to violate the laws of God, your maker. You have no built-in "right" for sexual fulfillment.

Another version of this lie says, "I am controlled by my needs. Surely a loving, generous God understands my needs and wants me to be fulfilled and happy." This is a distortion because God's primary goal in your life is not your happiness but your holiness. God knows that only in holy living can happiness be genuinely produced. But here you are consumed with a desire to have your needs met and your rights met, and you fall into the satanic strategy of sabotage. God will meet your needs if they are legitimate. If you actually had an inescapable need for sex outside of marriage as a single adult, and it was a need you could not live without, God would have provided for it legitimately. The same Bible that says, "And my God will meet all your needs according to his glorious riches in Christ Jesus" (Philippians 4:19, NIV) is the same Bible that has always prohibited any sexual activity outside of marriage. Be careful not to fall into the satanic trap of being so consumed with your needs that you forget the God who can meet them in right ways, not wrong.

THE ROOTS OF TEMPTATION

Temptation is able to take root in your life in three areas:

1. Unresolved needs. This is a particular problem for women. Women are more vulnerable to sexual temptation when they are unsatisfied with the level of intimacy in their marriages. As we saw in chapter 2, women need to communicate with their husbands on a deep emotional level. If a husband doesn't allow her into his thoughts and his life, then a wife can become emotionally starved. She may then search for a way to have this need met. She's not looking for sex but for intimacy. It is the opposite for a man.

If his wife is not responsive sexually over a long period of time, his need becomes fertile soil to grow the wicked plant of sexual temptation. In either of these situations, both parties may be at fault in creating the conditions in the marriage that lead to unresolved needs.

I'm not saying that every need in your life will be met and you won't be happy unless it is. That's just not true. You must learn discipline. I'm talking about unresolved needs—needs you and your spouse will not face nor seek help toward resolving.

2. Undisciplined desires. Your desire for great sex is not wrong—and God wants it fulfilled in a good, healthy marriage—but if you don't discipline your desire, it will wreck and ruin your life. That was one of the problems of Samson in the Old Testament. He never disciplined his desires. He wanted whom he wanted when he wanted with no restraint and discipline.

3. Preoccupation with yourself. When you become so preoccupied with selfishness that you want everything right now without discipline, it can be a real curse, financially and sexually. Temptation finds fertile soil in the self-centered heart of a man or woman who is so preoccupied with what he or she wants that he or she doesn't think of his or her spouse. If there is poor communication in the marriage, or unresolved needs, or undisciplined desires, these become time bombs in the selfish person. If you are content, you will not be frustrated or tempted.

SEXUAL SEDUCTION

Frustration fuels your temptation and sets the stage for sexual seduction. The book of Proverbs gives an excellent picture of the progression of sexual seduction that is equally applicable for men and women.

> I saw among the simple, I noticed among the young men, a youth who lacked judgment. He was going down the street near her corner, walking along in the direction of her house at twilight, as the day was fading, as the dark of night set in. Then out came a woman to meet him, dressed like a prostitute and with crafty intent. (She is loud and defiant, her feet never stay at home; now in the street, now in the squares, at every corner she lurks.) She took hold of him and kissed him and with a brazen face she said: "I have fellowship offerings at home; today I fulfilled my vows. So I came out to meet you; I looked for you and have found you! I have covered my bed with colored linens from Egypt. I have perfumed my bed with myrrh, aloes and cinnamon. Come, let's drink deep of love till morning; let's enjoy ourselves with love! My husband is not at home; he has gone on a long journey. He took his purse filled with money and will not be home till full moon." (Proverbs 7:7-20, NIV)

I want you to see the chilling, frightening progression of seduction. Follow this closely.

1. Flirtation. The seduction begins in verse 13 when "she took hold of him and kissed him and with a brazen face she said . . ." She coyly got his attention and began flirting. The first stage of seduction is when you begin to flirt with sexual involvement.

Let me give you a serious word of warning.

Flirtation, to be dangerous, does not have to be with another person. You may be flirting with suggestive, pornographic material. You may be flirting with loose and lewd conversation. You may be flirting with activities and situations that could lead to danger. Flirtation opens the door to sexual seduction.

My wife and I have had friends who would occasionally joke with each other flirtatiously. It seemed innocent; no harm was intended. On the surface nothing seemed wrong with it. But I have since concluded that there is no such thing as innocent flirtation or sexual kidding because there is always the potential for triggering further sexual involvement. It is not a joke! It is serious, and you need to guard your conversation. Do not create a situation that could become explosive later in your life.

Proverbs 6:25 has a further word on flirtation. "Do not lust in your heart after her beauty or let her captivate you with her eyes" (NIV). Flirtation is a look that lingers long enough for seduction to take roots. You are setting your own trap.

2. Flattery. Look at verse 15 of the passage in Proverbs: she said, "I came out to meet you; I looked for you and have found you!" Here is a woman flattering a young man, telling him she is thrilled to see him and it is wonderful just to look at him. This young man's ego is being built, and he is vulnerable to Satan's trap. Flattery is the next step of seduction.

If you are having any lack of communication

in your marriage, you need to be very careful at this particular point. A man or woman at work might notice your discouragement, become sensitive to your hurts, and begin to flatter you with attention and compassion. Be careful not to shift your desire for emotional support from your marriage partner to the person flattering you. You will always be drawn to someone who strokes your ego.

3. Finery. Finery is an old term for glamour. The seductress says in verse 16, "I have covered my bed with colored linens from Egypt. I have perfumed my bed with myrrh, aloes and cinnamon." It is an attractive picture. To guard against being seduced by glamour, you must watch where you get your information about sex. Television and movies present sexual situations outside of marriage in a glamorous, mysterious, exciting fashion, and it is easy to fall for the bait. Satan wants you to be so dazzled by the excitement that you do not see the danger. But he doesn't present the truth.

4. Feelings. The fourth step in the progression of seduction is that your feelings become involved; your emotions are engaged. Look at verse 18, "Come, let's drink deep of love till morning; let's enjoy ourselves with love!" Those are physical terms with emotional overtones. Flirtation gets your attention. Flattery involves your ego. Finery dazzles your sense of excitement. But Satan's whole purpose is to get you to the point where you become emotionally entangled. Then you cannot see straight. Your passions dominate, and you say, "I can't help it. I must have her!" or "I must have him!" The seduction is almost complete.

Have you ever talked to a man who is having an affair with another woman? Ask him, "Why in the world are you destroying your family? Why are you killing yourself emotionally and spiritually?" If he looks at you and says, "I can't help it!" then he is emotionally entangled.

5. *False freedom.* Satan gives you the illusion of false freedom. Verse 19 says, "My husband is not at home; he has gone on a long journey. He took his purse filled with money and will not be home till full moon." In other words, we are free to enjoy ourselves. There are no restraints because my husband, the authority, is absent.

In an earlier chapter in Proverbs that deals with sexual immorality, Solomon suddenly stops cold and says, "God is closely watching you" (Proverbs 5:21, TLB). God is watching. God's laws are at work. God's results are coming.

Whenever someone tries to convince you that this or that is the door to sexual freedom, remember something: Satan is a liar and one of his most vicious lies is to offer you freedom in anything. Do you know why? Because of all the things Satan may offer you, one thing he can *never* deliver is freedom. It is not his to give.

Seduction begins with flirtation, and you must not open the door. If you don't flirt with sin, none of the rest will happen. Flirtation starts the cycle of seduction.

THE DARK SIDE OF IMMORALITY

What is the dark side of immorality? What does Satan not want you to know? Here are the dark results of sexual immorality.

1. Deception. You become a deceiver. You start covering your tracks and lying. You once considered yourself a person of integrity and moral honesty, and now you suddenly find yourself so sucked into this temptation that you are covering your tracks. You try to pretend it is not happening, and you try to convince everybody that everything is all right. Proverbs 14:12 says, "There is a way that seems right to a man, but in the end it leads to death" (NIV).

In *Myth of the Greener Grass* (Tyndale, 1983), noted Christian counselor J. Allan Petersen tells of a man who came to see him for help. The man was involved with another woman and his wife was getting suspicious. Dr. Petersen said, "Why don't you drop it and ask God's forgiveness?" The man said, "Drop it? I just can't. She makes me so happy and meets my needs." He continued to give five or six reasons why it must be all right, when it is all wrong! Proverbs 5:3-4 says, "For the lips of an adulteress drip honey, and her speech is smoother than oil; but in the end she is bitter as gall, sharp as a double-edged sword" (NIV). Deception will never work.

2. Domination. Sexual immorality begins to control you. It dominates your thinking. It is a bondage to slavery. Proverbs 5:22 reads, "The wicked man is doomed by his own sins; they are ropes that catch and hold him" (TLB). You are entangled and you can't pull free. The harder you struggle, the tighter your trap becomes. You are hooked.

3. Destruction of spiritual sensitivity. I wish with all my heart that none of this applied to God's people, but that is seldom the case. I hear sexual looseness in your conversation. Some of you are flirting with disaster and pumping things into your minds that are sexually suggestive. Your appetite for God starts to grow dull. Your perception of spiritual truth begins to diminish. You can listen to an anointed man of God Sunday after Sunday, carry your Bibles to Sunday school, and still get deeper and deeper into immorality. It is deadening. I read recently that it is popular in our culture not to speak of adultery but of having an affair. The word *affair* sounds more mysterious, romantic, exciting.

4. Degradation. Sexual immorality lowers your self-esteem. Satan is a master of trickery, right? Do you see how he begins with seduction and uses flattery and then actually degrades you? Lamentations 5:16 says, "The crown has fallen from [my] head. Woe to [me], for [I] have sinned!" (NIV). The crown is in the dirt because of my sin.

5. Damage. You damage your family, damage

your children, damage your friends. Numbers 32:23 says, "You may be sure that your sin will find you out" (NIV). And Proverbs 11:29 says, "He who brings trouble on his family will inherit only wind" (NIV).

ESCAPING TEMPTATION

I want to warn you about reading something like this and being smug, thinking, "I don't have to worry about seduction. I am strong." That is when Satan strikes. Do not become so comfortably proud of your spiritual maturity that you are a sitting duck for Satan's weapons. Don't think that this cannot happen to you.

My method for coping with seduction is to run scared. I don't take any chances. I don't walk into circumstances that I know will hurt me. I don't expose myself to material that is going to make it hard for me to obey God and be faithful to my wife. A great mark of spiritual maturity is to take the advice of the apostle Paul in 2 Timothy 2:22 and run from temptation. Or take the example of Joseph in Genesis 39 when he faced the allurements of Potiphar's wife: he turned his back and ran. Don't take chances with what can damage your life. So let's go over some things that will help you get out from under the gun of temptation.

1. Discuss. You need to discuss your temptations with someone you trust. If you can talk with your husband or wife, that's great. It will draw you closer together when you can discuss your temptations. If you can't do that, pray that God will develop closeness between the two of you. Until that happens, find a friend who will guard your confidence.

2. Pray. If you don't know Jesus Christ as your Savior, praying will do you no good. The Bible says that without Jesus Christ, the spiritual part of you is dead and can only come alive when you receive Jesus Christ as your Savior through his death on the cross. But when that happens, you have an incredible power in prayer. You need to be honest with God. He knows anyway. God won't be shocked. He knows what you think and you need to tell him.

3. Study. You need to study the negative effects of your temptation. Study what could happen to you if you follow through with this. You don't need to think about how great it would be to sleep with him or to sleep with her. You need to think about what would happen to your wife or husband or to your children. What about your walk with God, your self-respect, or your business?

4. Expose. You need to expose the temptation itself the moment you think about it. The moment the temptation comes into your mind, do not tuck it away in the back of your brain. Expose it immediately as a temptation. "I know what you are. You're my enemy. You will kill me." Expose it clearly.

These four things will be the result:

1. You will lower your frustration level. Frustration is what gives temptation its power.

2. You will come closer to actual solutions. Temptation thrives in your imagination. Sexual sin will not solve any of your problems, it will only create more severe difficulties. You need to come closer to real solutions. Resolve your needs. Discipline your desires. Don't be occupied with yourself. Occupy yourself by serving God and other people.

3. You weaken the power of temptation. It is no longer the secret thing that is haunting you. Now it is out in the clear sunshine of God's standards, and temptation can't live in the sunlight.

4. You will build accountability. You now have accountability to God and the person with whom you have shared. It will protect you, strengthen you, give you a great sense of confidence that you can handle it. Someone else is on your side. Above all, avoid secrecy. Remember that frustration and temptation grow in secret. Bring temptations out into the light and expose them for what they are. The two most deadly thoughts in facing temptation are *I can get away with it,* and *No one will ever know.*

God suspends the rules of life for no one. You can be sure that your sin will find you out. Galatians 6:7-8 says, "Do not be deceived: God cannot be mocked. A man reaps what he sows" (NIV). Sowing the wrong principles will reap the wrong results.

FREEDOM FROM TEMPTATION

I want to wrap this up by saying something very special. The solution to the sexual temptations of this generation is very simple. And that solution is tough-minded choice.

1. *Choose to know God through Jesus Christ.* He said, "I am the door. No man comes to the Father but by me." You need to choose Joshua 24:15. Joshua said to a very rebellious generation, "Choose for yourselves this day whom you will serve. . . . But as for me and my household, we will serve the Lord" (NIV). Choose Jesus Christ and his cross and his death for you as your Savior.

2. *Choose right living.* You don't have to give into garbage. You don't have to read certain magazines. You don't have to spend time alone with certain people. You can choose right living. Jesus Christ can and will give you the power to do it. Without Jesus Christ, it is just a lot of hard work. A lot of religions in the world believe that you get right with God through working hard to please God and then hoping you'll make it—but you're never sure you will. If you allow Jesus Christ to come into your life through his Holy Spirit, he'll take up a powerful residence inside of you. He said, "I stand at the door and

86

knock. If anyone hears my voice and opens the door, I will come in and eat with him, and he with me" (NIV). He will give you inner power to change your life. And then you can commit yourself to right living. Ephesians 5:6-8 says, "Let no one deceive you with empty words, for because of such things God's wrath comes on those who are disobedient. Therefore do not be partners with them. For you were once darkness, but now you are light in the Lord. Live as children of light" (NIV). You can choose right living.

3. *Choose committed love.* Listen to this in Ephesians 5:28-29, 33: "Husbands ought to love their wives as their own bodies. He who loves his wife loves himself. After all, no one ever hated his own body, but he feeds and cares for it, just as Christ does the church—for we are members of his body. . . . However, each one of you also must love his wife as he loves himself, and the wife must respect her husband" (NIV).

4. *Choose to accept God's rules of life.* We've talked a lot about sex. Here's a brief passage that indicates the power of obeying God's rules and the foolishness of disregarding them, Proverbs 5:3-5: "For the lips of an adulteress drip honey, and her speech is smoother than oil; but in the end she is bitter as gall, sharp as a double-edged sword. Her feet go down to death; her steps lead straight to the grave" (NIV). You never go wrong obeying the laws of God, and you will not and cannot win by disregarding them.

God wants you to have a whole, healthy, happy life. Giving into sexual temptation is the road to death and destruction. God can forgive you, you can be restored, you can come back, but you will carry scars for life. You will harm your children unbelievably, you'll devastate your husband or wife, and the people who trust you. You will violate trust if you fail to be godly.

Maybe you have already failed, and you are feeling sick right now because you know the harm and damage, and you can't get away from it. But the Bible says that God will take your sin as far from you as the east is from the west, and that means they will never meet again. He will drop them into the sea of his divine forgetfulness. When you are forgiven, you are totally forgiven. You may still face the penalties in this life, but God can bring you to a restoration beyond anything you have ever known. A loving God can still heal and help you, and he is your only hope for that kind of restoration.

If you are facing temptation, do not give in to it. Get the frustration out in the open, resolve your needs, let God replace your selfishness with love for him and love for other people. And get right in the areas we've covered. Become healthy, well balanced, and well adjusted. Work on the quality of your marriage. Take your frustrations out of their hidden, private soil, and come into the sunlight of God's help. Let God develop a healthy marriage in your relationship.

And I mean this when I say it: God bless you!

FIVE
STRESS IN THE FAMILY

There was a time when Amy told me she had become stressed in our marriage, our ministry, and our traveling. "You are the reason," she said to me. "You are the fault." I had dumped so much negative stuff on her for such a long span of time that my wife, who is vibrant, beautiful, and full of vitality, had begun to lose her wonderful free spirit. So, one night we prayed long and hard. I realized I had been producing stress for Amy, and that night was a turning point. God helped me begin to relax and enjoy a calmer spirit of trust in him. I made a deliberate decision to stop pouring stress onto my wife.

Your home should be a retreat, a place to let down and unwind, a place where you know you are unconditionally loved. But if you see your family as designed to meet your deficiencies and to make up for the stress outside your home, you will succeed only in bringing stress into your home. If you perceive that your spouse exists for your comfort, then you are a very self-centered, selfish person! You need to grow up in your marriage. You need to learn to love the other person. He or she doesn't exist just to make you happy.

The Bible speaks of the law of reciprocity—giving and receiving—and it pertains to more than just money. If you are a constant taker, you end up a shriveled, empty person. But if you are a giver, it comes back to you unexpectedly, powerfully, wonderfully. If you show love to your family, teach them positive principles, and lead them to Jesus Christ, then you are building them up. And they in turn will build, support, and encourage you. It is a law of life.

I am not saying that your family should not help you. They certainly should. Sometimes you will need to come home and say, "I can't handle it. Help me." And they will love and help you. But if you're a constant taker, not a giver, then you are in trouble.

STRESS AND MARITAL SEX
Stress can enter a marital relationship when one spouse expects more from sex than it can deliver. One of the greatest things in the world is God's gift of sex to be enjoyed between one man and one woman in a committed marriage. But you cannot expect more from sex than it can deliver. If you try to make sex do too much in your marriage, you will create stress. Sex is a

way of expressing love, a way of bonding to one another, a way of deepening intimacy and commitment. Sex is not a problem solver, and jumping in and out of bed will not solve your problems of debt, in-laws, child rearing, or illness. Many husbands and wives who speak to me privately have problems with sexual maladjustment because one spouse is too demanding and expects sex to be a problem solver.

Some people have grown up with negative attitudes about sex and have been taught that sex is dirty and unclean. One man I met with this problem could not even begin to show the right kind of physical love to his wife for the first three years of their marriage. This affected her self-esteem; she felt something was wrong with her, and it created stress in their relationship.

If you are having a lot of stress in this area, get some help from a counselor. Ask God to help you. Remember that if a husband pressures his wife, she will withdraw. And if a wife hides from the problem or resents her husband in this area, the stress will only get worse and intimacy will erode. God did not make a mistake when he gave the gift of sex to married couples. He meant it to be a wonderful joy and a great bonding between two people. If it is not this for you, seek help.

PRESCRIPTION FOR SEXUAL HEALTH
Here are four prescriptions for sexual health in your marriage.

91

1. Have an attitude toward sex that is sane, balanced. This means that you recognize that sex is good because it comes from God, but you balance it with a realization that sex is only for marriage.

2. Sex is sustaining; it produces children. Let me remind you that Hollywood did not invent sexuality and should not determine your understanding of it. God created sex with a primary result being children.

3. Sex should be satisfying in a marriage. Satisfying here means a medium for intimacy, an open channel of warmth, loyalty, and communication. It is a psychological fact that you can communicate on a deeper level sexually than in any other way. For sex to be truly satisfying your whole person needs to be engaged tenderly in loyalty, intimacy, and contentment.

4. Sex should be sizzling. God intended sexual excitement. Do you sometimes feel your sexuality is a cross to bear and God made some kind of mistake? God knows what he is doing. If you are having any problem in this area, I suggest you carefully go through God's SOS for Christian marriage: the Song of Solomon. It is a beautiful description of married sexual love in the Bible. In chapter 1, the husband calls his wife "my love," and he's referring to sexual love. Then he uses the term "my darling." The Hebrew word means literally, "my darling, my sexual companion." In chapter 2, you will find an apple tree. In the Middle East, the apple tree was a symbol of sexual loving and skill between two partners in a marriage. Later in chapter 2 is the term "love sick," and the Hebrew means "intense sexual passion." This is a beautiful description of sexual love in a marriage. If you read the Song of Solomon in a modern translation, you will read of a young couple in love with each other. They never put each other down. They lavish affection and praise on each other. And throughout the Song of Solomon is the smile of God's approval.

CHILDREN AND STRESS

According to the National Pediatric Institute, the number one health problem for children today is stress. Stress in children! Much of that pressure comes from Mom and Dad. I have encountered situations where children were pushed to perform, not for the benefit of the child, but because the parents wanted to improve their own images.

Dr. David Elkind, a child psychologist in New England, has written two outstanding books about pushing children into maturity before they are ready for it: *The Hurried Child* (Addison-Wesley, 1981) and *All Grown Up and No Place to Go* (Addison-Wesley, 1984). In *The Hurried Child* Dr. Elkind quotes from an article by Susan Ferraro entitled "Hotsy Totsy":

> *It was a party like any other with ice-cream and cake, a donkey poster and twelve haphazard donkey tails, and a door prize for everyone, including*

Toby, the birthday girl's little brother who didn't do anything but smear icing. "Oh," sighed little seven-year-old Melissa, as she opened her first present. It was Calvin Klein jeans. "Oh," she gasped, as the second box revealed a bright new top from Gloria Vanderbilt. There were Christian Dior underpants from Grandma, a satiny little blouse and matching bloomer bottoms, and Mommy herself had fallen for a marvelous little party outfit from Yves St. Laurent. Melissa's best friend gave her a special sports shirt complete with the right insignia on the front. Added to that were a couple of books, and all of the gifts were much appreciated except for the fancy doll that one guest's mother insisted on bringing to the seven year old. (American Way Magazine, April 1981, 11)

Do you see the pressure here? I'm not saying that you are wrong for giving your children designer clothes, but situations like this are repeated all over America where children are expected to grow up quickly. Let's look at the kind of pressure children are under.

Academic Pressure
Children are being pressured to learn things much too early, and they feel stress because of it. Recent studies have revealed that it may be negative in the long run for a child to be pressured to read too early (Elkind, *Hurried Child*). Some parents want their child to be able to read at three, four, or five years of age, and that's fine if the child wants to read. But if you are pressuring your child so your image will grow, then you are creating unnecessary stress. According to one study, a child who masters basic reading

94

skills as late as seven years of age attains the same reading level in a year or two as a child who learned to read at five or six. But by the time these same children are in junior high and high school, the child who learned later likes to read more than the child who was pressured into learning. I'm not trying to make anyone feel guilty if he has a young reader. Your child may love to read the rest of his life. But if you are putting pressure on him to learn everything early, you may be stressing him beyond his level of development.

I'm not an expert in this area; I'm not a child psychologist nor a medical professional. I'm merely quoting different studies that deal with stress and children. Realize that you may be putting small children under great academic pressure to make you look better as a parent.

Sports Pressure

Another area of pressure for children is sports. They have tremendous pressure to excel in Little League. I watched a newscast recently that showed a videotape of a Little League game. The umpire ruled against a certain child on a team, and a parent attacked the umpire, striking him repeatedly. Other parents soon joined in and mobbed the umpire. And this happened in a middle-class neighborhood. I know that is extreme, but I have talked to children who get physically sick because they fear they are not measuring up to their parents' standards in athletics, and they are only six, seven, and eight years old. I want to warn you of the stress you can produce in your kids.

Social and Sexual Pressure
According to Dr. Elkind, the pressure for children to be cool is so great that "when the rattle goes in the mouth, the foot goes on the social ladder." Social and sexual pressure are related. I have been deeply offended by television commercials that portray children in sexual situations. Some of the commercials for blue jeans are particularly bad. These commercials put elementary and junior high children in sexually explicit situations and make them act very seductive. This makes me angry because it is exploiting these children.

Why put so much stress and pressure to perform on your child so that growing up is no longer fun? Suicide is one of the leading killers of teenagers in this country. The most affluent suburb of Chicago has the highest teenage suicide rate in Illinois and almost the highest in the entire country. You need to teach your children discipline, character, and hard work, but do so without extreme stress and pressure. My daughter, Allison, is seven years old, but she has been learning for a couple of years that if she is to get something, she has to earn it. She's excited about that. She earns pennies, nickels, and dimes, and they're adding up. We are also teaching her the principles of giving, tithing, and saving. She is learning important principles for life, but at the same time we want her to be a kid as long as possible. I don't want her to face adult stress—she's not ready yet.

This is difficult stuff to hear, and some of you may be angry at me for saying these things. But I am talking about loving your children. Will you think about it? Will you pray about it? Today's kids are living with loads of pressure—status, academics, athletics, sex. Sometimes the stress is just more than a child can handle in the early stages of development. If your child has a natural interest in sports or academics and loves what he's doing, then he should be encouraged in these areas as long he balances his interests with his spiritual and social growth. But beware that a lot of children involve themselves in things because they fear that Mom and Dad will be disappointed if they don't. Some of this is part of a child's learning his identity, but when it becomes a stressful situation and affects his self-esteem because your ego as parent is involved, then you are creating unnecessary stress. You must have greater concern for the welfare of your child than for your own image.

SIX
SELFISHNESS

Some months ago my wife and I were making preparations for a family life conference in Chattanooga. While I was in the process of preparing, I received a phone call from a reporter at a local newspaper. She said she had received special permission to do a major article on our coming to Chattanooga, and she wanted some vital information. She interviewed me for nearly an hour, and we talked about what I believed God wanted to see accomplished in this crusade. At the end of the interview, she had a question for her personal interest: "What is the most serious marital problem in America? I have asked several people—marriage experts and seminar leaders—this same question and they have all repeatedly emphasized communication. What do you think?" I paused for a moment and said, "I believe that communication is the most mechanically serious problem in marriage, but I am thoroughly convinced that the most serious problem is ordinary selfishness." Communication problems are often an expression of selfishness because at the root of any relationship problem is selfish motivation.

I want to make something clear. When you do not know Jesus Christ personally, when he is not in charge of your life, you are motivated and controlled by selfishness. Ecclesiastes 9:3, a shocking verse, reads, "The hearts of men [and women], moreover, are full of evil" (NIV). You are driven by selfish patterns. Even when you do know Christ personally, and he is living in you, you still will have those moments when you lapse into self-centeredness.

THE RESULTS OF SELFISHNESS

I want to give you a list of what happens in your life when you allow it to be controlled by selfishness.

1. Shrunken personality. When you allow selfishness to run the show, you have a shrunken personality. You become a little person. If you are driven by the winds of self-centeredness, then you find your character beginning to shrink and shrivel. You become occupied with pettiness.

2. Insecurity. When you are driven by selfishness and dominated by self-centeredness, you breed insecurity in yourself. For example, in your job or career you may believe that the best way to achieve is to assert yourself and be aggressive no matter who gets in your way. You justify this kind of action by saying, "This is the way any company operates." You come across as tough as nails and you project an image of being so strong. But while you are selfishly climbing a ladder of career success, you are breeding terrible insecurity, always looking over your shoulder to see who is watching you or who is after your position.

3. Irresponsibility. Selfishness increases an attitude of irresponsibility. This is a colossal problem in modern America especially for men. We are living in a generation of father failure: men abandon responsibility for their families by withdrawing emotionally or walking out physically. I talk to men frequently who can look me straight in the eye and admit that they rarely see their children or take any emotional responsibility for them. One man had just gone through a very painful divorce. He said, "I have not seen my daughters since the divorce and I rarely pray for them. I figure they are better off with their mom, and it is better if we get that part of our lives behind us." This is a man who knows Christ, is responsible for his children, helped bring them into this world, and is now acting irresponsibly.

I have counseled women who have walked out on their families because they wanted personal freedom, breaking the hearts of children and leaving them in total confusion, shattered because their moms had to clutch an illusive dream of freedom.

This irresponsibility builds pressure to walk out, quit, say forget it. Selfish people need wake up to their responsibilities.

4. *Isolation.* When you allow selfishness to really control your life, you can build a situation where you drive people from you. You want to selfishly clutch at them, making sure they stay close. But your jealousy dominates them and you get the opposite effect: you drive them away from you and suffer isolation and loneliness.

I did some research into a very influential, turn-of-the-century family who lived in Connecticut. The woman, Isabella, and her husband, John, a successful attorney, lived in Litchfield and were prominent in the social, political, and economic circles of their part of the country. As I read the history of the family, I came across a fascinating section that said Isabella's major problem in her family was her total possessiveness of her two daughters. Early on, Isabella had determined she would do anything in her power to force her daughters to stay at home in the community of Litchfield. She pressured them, pushed them, and loaded all kinds of guilt onto them so they would marry young men from Litchfield and settle there permanently. But her two daughters married attorneys and moved as far away as they could. This woman drove the people she loved away from her life because of trying to hold them by force.

5. *Sadness.* If you live your whole life demanding what you want, you will eventually find

yourself a victim of the sickness of sadness, because nothing is more lonely or more sad than a person who has lived selfishly. I know a man who has lived most of his life selfishly. He has never been very generous or giving. He has always been rather harsh with his family and stern with his children. This man is now getting near the end of his life and nobody loves him. He is sick with sadness.

I met another man in Pennsylvania who came to me after a service. He said, "Ron, I destroyed my children. They no longer want to be with me. I have been so strict and cruel, and I have done it all in the name of God. I have tried to force them to live a certain way to make sure they never caused me any embarrassment or trouble. Now my children cannot wait to get away from me. And I am sad!"

This is not the way you want to live—nor do you have to. You can choose to transfer control of your life from yourself to Jesus Christ. He is the source of miraculous change.

WHEN JESUS CHRIST CONTROLS YOUR LIFE
We've looked at the results of selfish living. But what happens when Jesus Christ controls your life? Let me show you five things.

1. *You become more like him.* That is incredible, isn't it? Romans 8:29 says, "For from the very beginning God decided that those who came to him—and all along he knew who

would—should become like his Son, so that his Son would be the First, with many brothers" (TLB). This is a promise that God will take your personality and fit it to the image of Jesus Christ. You are going to become like a photograph of Jesus Christ. This does not mean, incidentally, that when Christ rules you, he obliterates your personality. He *fulfills* your personality and that is much different. When Jesus really controls you, you become progressively like him. That is an incredible realization. To understand what this means, I suggest you study the gospels, paying particular attention to the way Jesus treated people.

2. Your ability to love people is enlarged. It is amazing how many men and women know Jesus but cannot love. Christ wants to reach into your life supernaturally with hands of healing and begin to unclog the channel of your ability to love.

3. Your self-esteem increases. When Jesus Christ really rules your life, he builds your self-esteem. You always thought that looking out for number one was the secret. You had to walk on other people. You had to climb the ladder of success and assert yourself. But that only results in insecurity, loneliness, and guilt. When you choose God's way of loving and caring for people, it strengthens your self-esteem.

4. Your tensions will be reduced. When Jesus rules your life he will ease the tension that selfishness produces. He will ease the stress that comes from living selfishly. It is tough to be self-centered because you create tension. You produce division in your family, in your work. Jesus lowers the tension level because he removes the selfishness.

5. *You will draw others to Christ.* When Jesus is excitedly in charge of your life, he will make you a broadcaster of spiritual attractiveness. You will become a godly magnet. There is a powerful phrase in the book of Psalms: "the beauty of holiness." It is speaking of the attractive beauty of holy living.

Charles Swindoll, in his book entitled *Growing Strong in the Seasons of Life* (Multnomah, 1983), talks about how people who do not know Jesus perceive those of us who do. He says we are often perceived as judgmental, harsh, opinionated, hard-to-live-with people; the reason is because we are that way. I believe it is satanic that our image to the world is that of sour sadness and harsh judgmentalism. It is true that we must take a bold stand for godly truth without reservation. But we must do it in the fantastic tenderness of Christ. If we don't, we obliterate our witness.

THE SEVEN SIGNALS OF SELFISHNESS

We have seen the results of living a selfish life and the results of a Christ-controlled life. If you have a good degree of spiritual intelligence, then you want Jesus to be in charge. Now let's look at seven signals that indicate a selfish spirit is ruling in your life.

1. *You are overoccupied with your needs, rights, and fulfillment.* We live in a time where this is top priority. Everyone is screaming, "Give me my rights, give me my needs, give me my fulfillment." We are living in a generation that mass murders thousands of unborn children for the sake of convenience and *rights.* "It's my right to privacy," a woman says. But as she talks about her right of choice she is really talking about convenience, selfishness, and sin. You do not get fulfillment by demanding it. You do not gain it by pursuing it.

The Bible speaks about seeds falling on the ground, dying, and then producing fruit—that is God's principle. You gain fulfillment by dying to your own rights and needs and letting Jesus Christ rule your life.

2. *You become depressed or angry when you do not get what you want.* You may lose your temper and blow up. Or you may become depressed or quiet—a martyr. Some psychologists believe depression is really a form of unresolved anger, and it may result because you did not get what you wanted.

3. *You have a bitter attitude toward life.* You may be able to give me a thousand reasons why you deserve to be bitter. You can tell me all the horrible things people have done to you and even how God has disappointed you. You may be the innocent victim of someone else's sin. But if

you choose to continue in your bitterness, cutting yourself off from God, blaming others, and refusing to get help toward resolving your feelings, then selfishness is the root of the problem. If you look closely you may discover that you even enjoy your bitter attitude toward life because of the control it gives you over others. You are creating a huge roadblock that is keeping God's love from penetrating and healing you and setting you free.

4. *You seek to control other people.* Notice I did not say you seek "authority" over other people. I am talking about wanting power. How many marriages are subtle, or not so subtle, power struggles? Some of you may feel it is the only way to get ahead in your marriage. Whenever you are seeking power over another person, you cannot fully love and respect that person.

5. *You have a critical tongue.* Some of you may be emotional bullies and you try to verbally batter others into submission. A few months ago, a woman told me that her husband had never physically abused her and had always provided money for her, but her marriage was a wreck because she had lived with verbal abuse for thirty years. A critical tongue pursues arguments all of the time.

Remember the verse in Proverbs that describes a woman verbally battering her husband: "A nagging wife annoys like constant dripping" (Proverbs 19:13, TLB). The drops keep coming until it nearly drives you crazy. A critical tongue that pursues and provokes arguments is a definite sign of a selfish spirit.

6. You are unable to admit wrong and apologize. Or if you do admit it, it is amazingly tough. I began establishing a pattern with my daughter when she was two and a half. I knew she would not understand logically what I was doing, but I wanted to set the pattern. I had done something, and I do not recall what it was, but I had been unfair to her. I went to Allison, got down in front of her, and said, "Allison, you don't understand this, but your daddy was wrong and I want to apologize. Will you forgive me?" She looked at me very blankly. So I said, "Say yes!" And she said, "Yes."

Some day I will need her forgiveness, and she will know that I am genuinely sorry for what I did. I am asking God to help me learn to do this now with a daughter who is the treasure of my heart. Do you think your pride and ego that makes you unable to apologize and ask forgiveness really produces good in your life? Do you feel if you ask your children for forgiveness that your authority will go down the tube? The opposite is true: their respect for you will become gigantic! They will see that you are genuine in your surrender to Christ and your love for them.

7. You become lazy in your relationships. In an earlier chapter I mentioned the serious and much-needed conversation Amy and I had around our eleventh anniversary. Although we had had a wonderful marriage for ten years,

Amy and I realized something was wrong. I was very occupied in building a ministry I believed God had brought me to, and I was becoming very lazy in developing the quality of my marriage.

As a man it is easy to pour your heart into building a career, but do you put that amount of emotional energy into your family? Wherever you focus your energy is your priority. You get a lot more ego fulfillment from your job than you do from your preschool child. You need to decide against ego fulfillment so you do not become lazy in your relationships and because of selfishness miss the quality of your marriage and family life.

FREEDOM FROM SELFISHNESS

What do you do to be free of self-centered motivation?

1. Make certain that Jesus Christ really is Lord of your life. Galatians 2:20 says, "I have been crucified with Christ: and I myself no longer live, but Christ lives in me. And the real life I now have within this body is a result of my trusting in the Son of God, who loved me and gave himself for me" (TLB).

2. Learn with God's help to relax your relationships. Are you tough on people? Are you hard to live with? Don't be so hard on your kids. Enjoy them. In Matthew 7:1, Jesus said, "Do not judge, or you too will be judged" (NIV). The word

109

judge here literally means don't allow yourself to be the judge, the jury, and the executioner.

Don't be so bothered if people don't do it just the way you want. Sometimes it is not spiritual things you are trying to help them learn. It is just your own petty preferences. Relax! Learn to love people. John 13:35 says, "Your strong love for each other will prove to the world that you are my disciples" (TLB).

3. Be a doer of love, not a feeler. Don't wait to feel it, do it! First Corinthians 13:4-7 is a list of love verbs. It is a famous passage on love, and yet there is not one phrase about feeling love anywhere in it!

4. Commit yourself to a giving life-style. Luke 6:38 says, "For if you give, you will get! Your gift will return to you in full and overflowing measure, pressed down, shaken together to make room for more, and running over. Whatever measure you use to give—large or small—will be used to measure what is given back to you" (TLB). And why is it that we apply that verse exclusively to money? Jesus is talking about general giving as a life-style—time, emotion, love, and talent. Here we have the awesome generosity of God through Jesus Christ dying a brutal death on the cross for us. What better example do we have to make us generous for him? The happiest people in the world are those who know Jesus and are giving.

A giving life-style is not natural for me. I was an only child and while I was growing up, most activity revolved around my desires. But making the commitment to give has been crucial to my own growth. God has had to mature me beyond my self-centeredness to Christ-controlled giving. This has been essential to my happiness and the happiness of those with whom I live. Commit yourself to a giving life-style. It is always better to be a giver than a taker.

SEVEN
PRESSURE FROM PARENTS

Most of the people I have met operate on one of two levels: they are either driven by their parents or they are haunted by them. We are all a product of our parents, for good or bad. We are a product of a complex set of growing experiences. Some of us have received vital and precious material from our parents that has enabled us to be all that we are today. Others of us are succeeding today in spite of our parents. Still others have labored for years with tremendous bitterness, great resentment, and tremendous hostility toward our mothers and fathers.

I'm in my late thirties, and every year I come to new discoveries of how my mom and dad have affected me for good or bad: how they have done great good for me and how I have tried to unlearn some things from them. And I do not mean that disrespectfully. I want you to focus carefully on your own relationship with your parents or your relationship with your children or grandchildren. Because if there are dangerous, destructive, unhealthy patterns, they must stop, and they must stop now! If you are harming your children, stop. If you are pouring into your children attitudes that create tremendous tension for them, that must also stop. And if you are on the receiving end of tension and hostility and stress, then you need to find God's way to come to peaceful terms with your parents so that you can operate not on the basis of resentment and hostility but with a workable, healthy adult relationship that will honor Jesus Christ.

Some months ago, my wife and I were having lunch at a beautiful marina in New Jersey. As we sat there, a very fashionably dressed lady in her forties came in with a much older gentleman. They sat at a table right next to us, and I watched carefully the unfolding drama. You could see the tension developing between them. I overheard the woman telling this man that she thought this table would be acceptable. He did not think so at all and complained bitterly, saying he did not approve of this place, did not like the table, did not want to eat there. The lady struggled to maintain her composure. After five or six minutes, he abruptly stood up and left the dining room. She hurriedly followed him out. As we were leaving, I saw them again and they were arguing. By this time you have probably guessed that this was her father. She said to him, "Dad, why can't it ever work between us? Why can't we ever have a good time enjoying each other? All I wanted to do was have lunch with you. It has never worked. Do you think it ever will?" I could feel the pain and anguish in this woman as she said, "Dad, won't it ever work between us?"

God's way can make these relationships work. You may be carrying a gigantic load of resentment, and it is time to let God heal it. You need to come to terms with your parents.

MARKS OF AN UNHEALTHY RELATIONSHIP

Next we're going to look at seven marks of an unhealthy relationship with your parents. Then I want to give you seven scriptural ways to have a right relationship with your parents. The following descriptions are the effects of parental pressure primarily in your own life, but you may recognize elements of yourself as a parent as well.

1. Controlled by compulsiveness. The first mark of unhealthy pressure from parents is that you have a tendency to be controlled by compulsiveness, especially compulsiveness to follow the rules of your parents whether they are your rules or not. This compulsion may show in the way you act when you are with your parents. It is a tug backward to old ways.

I read recently the account of a thirty-two-year-old woman named Margaret, a successful journalist in New York, who went every two months to visit her parents in Connecticut. She dreaded each visit. Her dad was a very passive man who did not become involved emotionally in the family. Her mother was the dominant, critical force, always negative toward the father and making life miserable for him. Margaret finally determined that she would not be pulled into the old compulsive patterns of joining with the mother in being critical of her father, as it brought continual stress to her family. On her next visit, she walked in the door, and her father said hello. She told him she wanted to talk with him. He was startled but agreed to talk after his television program ended. She sat down to watch it with him, again to his amazement.

Soon Margaret's mother called from the kitchen asking Margaret to help her. And, knowing this was her first major test, Margaret answered that she was going to visit with her father. Total silence came from the kitchen. Ten minutes passed. Five more minutes passed. Margaret was having the most positive conversation with her father in her recent memory. Finally her mother's voice came from the kitchen, again asking for help. Margaret put her off, saying she wanted to talk to her dad. Two minutes passed, then a dish crashed. The mother called desperately, saying she'd cut her hand and needed Margaret's help. At this point the father looked at Margaret and told her to help her mother. Margaret encouraged her father to help his wife, but he urged Margaret to do it.

Margaret had succeeded well up to this point; but at her father's words she totally gave up.

She walked into the kitchen, noticed the small scratch her mother had, and bandaged it. For the next hour she found herself slipping back into the old patterns. She left in disgust. She concluded her story by saying that she does not dislike her parents, but dislikes herself when she is with them [Howard Halpern, *Cutting Loose: An Adult Guide to Terms with Your Parents* (Bantam, 1978)].

Old patterns are tough to break. Compulsive behavior controls you.

2. Pushed by perfectionism. I am not talking about doing your best. Doing your best is striving for excellence, putting your heart and soul into achieving. But perfectionism is an illusion that says if you don't do it perfectly, it is not worth anything; if you don't do it exactly right, there is something wrong with you. If you believe this about yourself, you are being ruled by impossible expectations. You cannot be perfect. The statement that builds perfectionism in children is "Can't you ever do anything right?" When a child hears those words repeatedly, he either retreats or determines to be perfect. If you find you are still being pushed by perfectionism as an adult, then you are caught in an unhealthy web of parental pressure.

3. Torn by tension. When you are torn by tension after contact with your parents, it is a dead giveaway that you are living in an unhealthy relationship of pressure. One well-known psychiatrist in New York said that the seven most common physical symptoms people report when they have had unhealthy, tense contact with their parents are headaches, breathing problems, suffocation, exhaustion, muscle spasms, difficulties with the colon, and lower back pain.

Do you find that contact with your mom or dad still leaves you wishing there was something stronger than aspirin? something to help you stop a splitting headache or breathe easier? This came home to me last year when I was leading a brief Bible study. A lady in her early thirties met me after a session and asked me to pray for her. She was very upset over time spent with her mother. What troubled her most was the effect the tension was having on her family. She didn't like the way she treated her husband after she had been with her mother, and her eight-year-old son had stomach problems every time his grandmother visited.

4. *Gripped by guilt.* Your parent makes you feel guilty. He or she moralizes everything. The common technique used in this kind of strategy is shame: you ought not, you should not. As an adult, your parents shame you in another way: "How could you do this to me? I gave you birth! I worked hard all my life! How can you treat me like this?" It totally stops anything rational, preventing you from praying with each other. The parent manipulates you through guilt into doing what he or she wants.

A moralizing parent is usually outraged at triviality. He or she may throw a fit because you stayed out all night on a date. Maybe you came home and were drunk. The parent is furious and for good reason. But here is the problem. The same parent who can be so outraged at something legitimately wrong can be just as outraged if you have not cleaned your room. Or you were supposed to practice piano for an hour and only practiced for fifty minutes. Everything is a moral wrong. Everything is a horrible sin, even if it is minor and trivial. It produces an oversensitive conscience. You are painfully sensitive, continually churning and producing more guilt than you can reasonably handle.

5. *Imprisoned at infancy.* When you are imprisoned or entrapped at infancy with your parents it means they still treat you like a baby. One fear a child has as he becomes an adult is that he will lose—or never earn—the respect of his parents. If you sense that Mom or Dad, who are gigantic figures in your life, don't respect you, you may feel you aren't worthy of respect. This can create tremendous fear that will enslave you at an infant level of responding to them—always trying to earn their respect.

6. *Jailed by judgmentalism.* If you grew up with critical, gossipy parents, you find these are learned traits. If your parents are always being negative and critical, always wounding and cutting verbally, attacking someone else, you can learn it. And what you may be doing as an adult is attacking your parents who taught you this. Remember this verse: "Fire goes out for lack of

fuel, and tensions disappear when gossip stops" (Proverbs 26:20, TLB).

7. Ripped by resentment. Your relationship with your parents rips you apart with resentment. Here is the problem: if you are a Christian and you know Jesus Christ personally, you may think that it is unspiritual for you to admit that you resent your parents. What does that accomplish? It merely makes you avoid the problem because suppressed resentment will always erupt some- where else. It is inevitable. You know you love your parents, but every time they call, you wince. You never face the problem, but you pay for it and your children pay for it. The resentment has an overall effect on your home and your life.

David Seamands, an author and our premari- tal counselor, recommended that we establish our young family with the use of two parent rugs that you lay on the floor. If your wife's parents have driven you crazy that week and you are try- ing to handle it, you go to the rug representing her parents and jump on it. And it works for the husband's parents too. This way you don't ever have to let resentment eat at you for something a parent does. This is a rather humorous way to deal with the problem, but you do have to deal with it. You cannot keep it bottled up.

SEVEN SOLUTIONS

The solution to parental pressure comes from the pages of God's totally true, wonderful book.

The reason it is so important is because unhealthy patterns will continue from generation to generation until someone has the courage to stand up and say, "Stop! I will not play this game anymore. I will not fight this battle anymore. I want to find God's way of solving this problem." Here are seven ways to solve unhealthy pressure.

1. Realistic view of God. You must operate first from a realistic view of God. Let's look at Luke 15, the famous account of the prodigal son. The word *prodigal* comes from a Greek word that means "wasteful, extravagant." Here was a young man who wasted his inheritance, embarrassed his family, humiliated his father, and then finally came to his senses. He started home expecting a difficult reunion with a dad he had left just a short time before. On the way to his father's house he rehearsed a speech in his mind: "Dad, I know what you are going to say. I know how you feel. I am wrong. No excuse. I don't expect you to treat me like a son. I don't deserve it. If you will just let me live in the servants' quarters, I will try to earn my way back. Give me a chance. I just want to see home again." As the son approached his family home, the father saw him a great distance away. At this point in the story, the first-century audience listening to Jesus was thinking, "Oh, boy, this kid is about to get it." They were waiting and watching. But Jesus surprised the crowd by saying, "The father stood up and ran to meet the boy. He embraced him, with total forgiving love, kissed his son, and said, 'Son, you are back. You are home! I love you.'"

Here is what is so startling. In the ancient world it was considered totally undignified for a grown man to run, and it was considered particularly undignified for a father to run to his child. That just was not done, but this father said, "Forget it!" and ran to his son.

What is the revealing truth of that story? The father is God. He is a loving God who wants to help you relate properly to your parents. He is not a God who is angry with you because of this trouble with your parents and is waiting to tear you to pieces. He is a God who wants to help you with this. He is a God who loves you. He is the God who runs to meet you. That is why, if you don't know the Lord Jesus, you need to come to him and accept his wide-open offer of incredible love—Jesus's death for you on the cross—and let God and his love be real in your life. Then you can learn how to relate to your parents and family in a right way. But you must start with a realistic view of God. You cannot win until Jesus Christ is Lord of your life.

2. Respect your parents. Ephesians 6:2 says, "Honor your father and mother" (TLB). The key word *honor* is a Greek word meaning literally "to give great weight or cost to something." Do you see the power of this? You respect your mom and dad even if they have lived wretched, godless lives. You still honor them as having great value. You are still able to say, "Mom and Dad, I love you, I honor you, I respect you, I give you great weight in my life. I value you."

3. *Recognize that your parents are human.* They are what they are. This means that some of you may need to drop feelings of disloyalty. Remember that it is not being disloyal to your parents to admit they are having problems or they are wrong. That is not disrespect. You must recognize this or it will create a great volcano of resentment and tear you to shreds.

Psalm 103:14 says, "For he knows how we are formed, he remembers that we are dust" (NIV). You are human. Sometimes you need to look your dad and mom squarely in the face and realize that it is not you causing the difficulty but some hurt within them. God knows that your parents are human, and you need to know this as well. Remember this: don't downgrade your parents but don't upgrade them either. Be realistic about them. Some of you have such an unrealistic view of your parents that you have to convince everybody that they are great, and you never face the problems that are tearing you apart. Just recognize that your parents are human.

4. *Learn to reject emotional blackmail.* Emotional blackmail says, "I will not love you unless you do this." You need to learn the godly way to reject emotional blackmail. Galatians 5:1 says, "It is for freedom that Christ has set us free. Stand firm, then, and do not let yourselves be

burdened again by a yoke of slavery" (NIV). Your parent may be using guilt, pressure, and criticism as conditions of love. If you don't learn to reject that emotional blackmail, you will probably produce the same patterns in your children, and the next generation will suffer.

5. *Release your expectations to God.* By this I mean both your parents' expectations of you and your expectations of them. You may be suffering from the "magic button" syndrome. It is the feeling that if you can just learn to push the magic button with your parents, it will all work. If you can just say the right thing, your dad will not act that way with you anymore. If you can get it right just once, your mom will not treat you like this. If you can just push the right magic button the problem will disappear. But this is such a false hope, and it keeps pulling you into disappointment. For most situations there is no magic button. You have to release your expectations to God or you will just keep getting hurt.

6. *Learn a right definition of independence.* I want to be very careful about this because there is a difference between independence and rebellion. It is a matter of your attitude. Ephesians 6:1-2 says, "Children, obey your parents; this is the right thing to do because God has placed them in authority over you. Honor your father and mother" (TLB). The key is the word *children.* The root in the Greek means "small, dependent children." So as an adult you are not scriptur-

ally obligated to obey your parents. You *are* under scriptural obligation to honor and respect them. You should still listen to your parents' counsel even if you do not agree with it.

Another example of right independence is from 1 Samuel 20. This passage gives the picture of a hot triangle of relationships: King Saul, his son Jonathan, and David. When David knew that Saul was going to kill him, he ran. Jonathan said, "David, you are mistaken. My father will not hurt you." David answered, "No, you are mistaken. I am not going back." So David hid and the night of the feast came. Saul asked, "Where is David?" Jonathan told his father that David was gone but would not tell him David's whereabouts. King Saul was furious and said, "Tell me, I command you." Jonathan refused. So King Saul threw a javelin at his own son. The Bible says Jonathan stood up in a great rage and rebuked his father, then left. The rest of the chapter makes it clear that God blessed what Jonathan did concerning his father.

Now I am not urging you to have a bad relationship with your parents. I'm trying to help you heal it. The Bible does not command you to live in blind obedience as adults. But it does command you to honor and respect. There is a difference.

7. Have prayerful rules and guidelines. This is true especially if it is a tough relationship. Set these guidelines after much prayer, after much time in the Word of God. Settle them in obedience to God. It may be that you say to your dad, "Dad, I love you, but certain things are off limits for us to talk about." Some of you may need to do what a pastor once told Amy and me: learn to love at a distance. You may decide to see your parents infrequently to avoid tension. The peace of your immediate family should be the determining factor. If your family is ripped apart by parental pressures, then you must stop it with God's loving help.

If you do not know Jesus Christ personally, your relationships can be so confusing. But a loving God says to come to his Son, Jesus Christ, and he will unlock the treasures and principles of his book, and you can know how to behave with your family.

EIGHT
GODLY MANHOOD

A few hours before King David knew he was going to die, he wanted to share something close to his heart with his son Solomon. It is a privilege to hear what a man says at this point in his life about what is most important to him. Let's look at this account in 1 Kings 2:1-3:

> When the time drew near for David to die, he gave a charge to Solomon his son. "I am about to go the way of all the earth," he said. "So be strong, show yourself a man, and observe what the Lord your God requires: Walk in his ways, and keep his decrees and commands, his laws and requirements, as written in the Law of Moses, so that you may prosper in all you do and wherever you go." (NIV)

David told his son to "show yourself a man." The same need is present for the men of this generation. I want now to open my own heart and lead you into a commitment to godly manhood.

While my wife and I were in Montgomery, Ala-

127

bama, a few years ago, we had a family life conference where God had done some tremendous
miracles. During the middle of the week, a lady
brought a special meal to us so we could relax,
and we talked with her for a while. About forty-
five minutes into the conversation, she shared
something that was painfully on her heart: "I
have a fourteen-year-old daughter with whom
we are having a terrible time. She is beginning to
rebel and we have done everything we can think
to do. We have prayed, examined the situation,
and talked to everyone we know. Do you have
any personal counsel for us?"

I had met her daughter during the week, and
God was beginning to do something very exciting in this young girl's life. I could sense she was
at a very important crossroad and needed serious direction. So I encouraged the mother to
have the father get the whole family together to
map out a strategy for helping this daughter.
The mother was very excited and asked for ma-
terials. We went over some information, and I
said to her, "Now you realize that it is crucial
that her father be vitally involved in this. In fact,
I urge you to have her father lead the discussion
because without his leadership you will not succeed." She blushed and said, "I don't think that
is possible. Her father loves her and he is a good
father, but I cannot count on him to be available
in something so emotional."

I saw immediately the root of failure in that
family: the father was not acting responsibly in

his role of family leadership. The man's role of leadership is so crucial. Whether the man is exercising the right leadership or not, he is still the major influence of the family. That family was experiencing the reversal of God's intentions of the family structure. This problem concerns me tremendously because every part of American society is threatened by the failure of men to take godly roles and godly leadership. Isaiah 3:12 says, "Youths oppress my people, women rule over them. O my people, your guides lead you astray; they turn you from the path" (NIV). This is a vivid picture of a society so completely out of order that it's paying a terrible price.

The role of men as family leaders does not lower the dignity of women one fraction. It does not eliminate the necessity for a woman to be a godly influence in her family. But there is one dominant, overriding principle that will control everything we are going to look at. If this important principle is violated, you and your family suffer inevitably. If it is followed safely, God will bless and honor it without any exception. The principle is this: men in every area of the life of the family are God's key to the spiritual and emotional welfare of the family. There is no exception to this statement. God expects men to exercise leadership and it is critical to do so.

From my counseling and speaking, I am aware that many men feel assaulted, attacked, and overwhelmed daily by forces that threaten to undermine their sense of manhood. Men are often fuzzy and unclear about their roles, and they respond by overreacting in one of three ways: (1) becoming passive and weak, giving in to other dominant forces, (2) becoming absorbed in their work, or (3) becoming super-macho tough men who try constantly to prove their manliness and virility. These three extremes are dangerous because they are distortions of God's accurate picture. What God says in his Word about male leadership shatters those deceptions and gives a clear picture of God's way to lead in a balanced way.

SPIRITUAL AND MORAL PROTECTION

Let's first look at the area of spiritual and moral protection. God's primary role of responsibility for men in a family or a church or a community is the role of spiritual and moral protection.

If you are a young man who is still dating, then God wants you to learn this lesson early. God expects you to be the moral and spiritual protector of the girl you date. You are to be her line of defense. Most young men have never heard or thought about this.

In order to be a protector, you need to have certain qualities.

1. Spiritual strength. You need deep, deep spiritual strength. It is obvious that you cannot have this strength until you know the Lord of strength, Jesus Christ. Some men are fighting a losing battle. You are trying to lead your family and you believe in male strength, but that is not the kind of strength God is talking about. It is not a strength of muscle but of godly character, and you cannot have this without the Lord Jesus in control.

2. Courage. You also need courage to be a man of integrity, a man of deep principle. I have had many men tell me they have lowered their convictions, eroded their standards, butchered their integrity in order to advance economically. If you do anything to violate your integrity, you have let the most precious thing in your life go down the drain. It is not worth it. Your family needs your direction here. You need the courage to resist the pressures that try to push you into compromising your principles. Your convictions need to be biblically centered. I am not urging you to have strong *opinions;* I am urging you to be a man of scriptural *convictions.* Your family needs it. You need it. Your neighbors need to see that kind of spiritual integrity even if it hurts you. You must have the courage to be a man of principle.

3. Decisiveness. You have to have the quality of decisiveness. I read a remarkable biography last summer about John R. Mott, a man few have heard of. He was the greatest student/ evangelist of the latter part of the nineteenth century. The mantle of D. L. Moody fell upon his shoulders after Moody's death in 1899. Mott came to the life-changing moment of his whole career when he was a student at Yale University.

He was going through the Yale library and found an old, dusty set of essays written by university presidents. One essay in particular caught his eye. It was entitled *Decisions of Character* and was written by the president of the University of Chicago. He read it looking to find the reasoning behind the title and finally found it in the concluding paragraph: "No decision you make is neutral. You need to determine early in your life that every decision you make will build character. You need to determine that every decision you make every day builds or destroys" [C. Howard Hopkins, *John R. Mott* (Eerdmans, n.d.)]. When Mott read that he realized God had spoken to him. He made a commitment as a young man that every decision he made for the rest of his life would be guided by God to build his character.

4. Trust in God. You need to train your family to trust in God in the midst of trouble and difficulty. In Psalm 44:17-18, David prays, "All this has happened, Lord, despite our loyalty to you. We have not violated your covenant. Our hearts have not deserted you! We have not left your path by a single step" (TLB). If you are going to protect your family, you must train them by example how to face trouble. Coming to know Jesus personally does not prevent trouble; you still have battle areas and problems to face. God uses many things to discipline you. You must learn how to face trouble the right way instead of losing your temper and caving in to the pressure.

I have a good friend who is a businessman in Atlanta. Last year he was on the edge of bankruptcy. He told me his story: "I got to the deepest, lowest emotional point in my life. I had been making a six-figure income, had done anything I pleased, had given to my church. The day came this past winter when I did not have enough money to buy groceries for my family. I was praying, searching God's Word, and wondering what in the world was wrong. We had come to a crucial moment in our family. I brought my two boys and my wife into our den. I knelt in front of my family and said, 'Boys, we are in financial trouble and we don't know where the grocery money is going to come from next week. I don't have any idea how we are going to get out of this, but I want you to know that God is going to take care of us. He will not fail to provide for us.' I asked my boys if they understood and they said, 'Yes, sir.' I said, 'Do you know that the finances are low?' They said, 'Yes, sir.' 'Do you know that God is going to take care of us?' And they said, 'Yes, sir. God is going to take care of us.'"

Within days, God was doing miracles. But do you know what the greatest miracle is? As those boys grow up and find themselves in trouble, will not go around the house kicking in doors. They will tell their wives and kids about when they were little boys and they trusted God and he rescued them. You must train your family to trust God.

5. *Be a guardian.* To protect your family

emotionally and spiritually, you must commit to be their guardian. I was praying about something in relation to this book, and I saw a very vivid picture. I saw myself as the father and husband of my family standing in the doorway of our home looking out at the worst enemies I could imagine facing our family: everything immoral, ungodly, and threatening ready to attack. And I stood there as one lone man. I believe with all my heart that you should stand in the doorway of your house, in a spiritual sense, and look all of those enemies squarely in the eye, and say loud and clear, "If you get into my family, you will have to get through me first." You are the guardian of your family.

6. *Fight false philosophies.* Finally, you are to fight against false philosophies that try to capture the thinking of your family. Proverbs 14:12 says, "There is a way that seems right to a man, but in the end it leads to death" (NIV). The majority of the material that floods your family comes under this verse. It looks right, but it is wrong. Your kids may have role models at school who are showing them unbiblical perspectives. You have erroneous material coming across the airways. I am shocked at the number of families we've counseled who have said, "We can't control what our kids watch on TV or the music they listen to." You can't afford to take that kind of position and let your kids get their morals from television. You are responsible.

A man from Kentucky told me, "Ron, I want to

help my kids, but I don't really like to study. I don't like to read. I am not comfortable with things like that. You are telling me to study the Word of God and to find out what my kids are thinking. And you are telling me to direct their mind patterns. I just don't think that is easy for me." Big deal! If you don't like to do these things, *learn to like doing them* because you must learn to direct your children's thinking. I pray to God every day that I will not be so mentally lazy that I fail to do the job of protecting my family by controlling what comes into their thinking. You have got to fight against false philosophies. You are the mental guardian of your family.

FINANCIAL PROVISION

The next major area is provision. You are to provide for your family. This does not mean that a woman cannot help economically, although I feel a deep concern about the masses of children in America who are getting their primary training in day-care centers. I do not believe day-care is God's pattern for society. Children need their parents. Some of you have economic struggles and time pressures that make the choice difficult, but it has to be a matter of priorities to put your children first.

There are two areas in which a man must provide for his family: financial and emotional. Some men accept their responsibility for the financial part but leave responsibility for the emotional side to women. But remember the principle? Men are the key in all areas. Let's first look at several steps to financial security.

1. *Be willing to work.* Romans 12:11 says, "Never be lazy in your work but serve the Lord enthusiastically" (TLB). You may have been programmed for failure economically, so when you get to the point that you are ready to succeed, you self-destruct. You don't provide for your family what God had in mind because you aren't willing to work for it.

2. *Control credit.* Proverbs 22:7 says, "The borrower is servant to the lender" (TLB). The reason many people have problems with credit is because they have been invaded with a subtle spirit of materialism. If you find you want material rewards right now without having earned them, this may your problem. You want many things, and you can't wait to get your hands on them. But to provide financial security for your family, you must control these desires and control your credit.

3. *Give gladly.* What kind of a witness is it to your family if you write out tithe checks, getting it to the last fraction, and then with a sigh of relief drop it into the offering plate, saying, "Well, I don't have to worry about that again for another month"? The Bible says in 2 Corinthians 9:7, "Each man should give what he has decided in his heart to give, not reluctantly or under compulsion, for God loves a cheerful giver" (NIV). If you begin as a cheerful giver, at some point

you'll become deliriously cheerful. It is tough at times, but God honors this.

I talked to a dentist in Indianapolis a few months ago who had never learned the principle of tithing. Recently, he sent a check for several hundred dollars to our organization, and I told him, "Jeff, you don't have to do this." He said, "No, I want to learn giving and God told me to give this." I said, "Listen, you don't have to send it to us." He said, "No, God is going to bless it and here is the first installment on my commitment." I said, "Well, what has happened so far?" He said, "I just gave it and I don't have any financial return yet, but God is doing miracles with my children." That is worth more than a big bank account.

EMOTIONAL PROVISION

Financial security is only half the picture. If all you provide are the basic necessities, you have essentially done no more than what an animal provides for its offspring. I don't mean to sound crude, but that is the plain truth. You need to provide emotional security beyond the finances. You do that in five basic ways.

1. Treat your family with tenderness and love. Ephesians 4:32 states, "Be kind to each other, tenderhearted, forgiving one another, just as God has forgiven you because you belong to Christ" (TLB). Do you remember everything you read a minute ago about decisiveness, strength, and courage? Do you get as turned on about tenderness and love or does that seem kind of weak? You need both together in a complementary way. Being tenderhearted does not short-circuit your strength. If all you have is strength, you will become harsh, biting, negative, critical, and judgmental of your own children.

2. *Tame your temper.* Ephesians 4:32 says, "Stop being mean, bad-tempered and angry. Quarreling, harsh words, and dislike of others should have no place in your lives" (TLB). One of the ugliest monsters in a marriage is a temper out of control. There is nothing manly about that. According to Galatians 5:22-23, one of the fruits of the spirit-controlled life is self-control.

I was speaking at a Christian academy in Dallas, Texas, to some senior-high students, and we had a question-and-answer time. A very attractive sixteen-year-old girl stood up and painfully shared the deepest battle of her life. She said, "I have such bitterness against my father. I want to love him and care for him, but I cannot bear another day of his embarrassing my mother. I cannot stand another moment of his yelling at us and attacking us." This father was a leader in the area, a church deacon, but he was terrorizing his family. You must tame your temper.

I prayed with a man in Montgomery, Alabama, and I respected him enormously. He came forward, but didn't shake my hand or anything. He just dropped to his knees and looked up at me and said, "I cannot hurt my family any more. I am a Christian, I made a commitment to Christ, but my temper is so out of control. Can God help me?"

God can, will, and wants to help you. But you must make a commitment.

3. Reinforce respect from your family. I am not talking about laying down the law and forcing your family to show you respect. Rather, reinforce an attitude on your part of respecting your family. Sometimes without realizing it, parents say things that put down and criticize their teenagers. If you want respect from your family, you need to treat them in the same way. Respect must be earned.

4. Lavish love and appreciation on your family. You cannot give too much of it. Let me give you an example. I was speaking at a ski retreat for some young people and we dealt with self-esteem. An eighteen-year-old boy came up to me and said, "I have never had a date in my life. My dad has never expressed appreciation to me for anything. Sometimes I would have just a little glimmer of excitement and I would think that maybe this time I had pleased him. But he would find something wrong and criticize me. And when I did something really good, he would say, 'Steve, don't worry. I know you can do better next time.'" That young man was having terrible battles believing he was worth anything because of the lack of appreciation from the most important person in his life.

Do you realize what a key a dad is emotionally? Every boy grows up with a hero image in his mind of the kind of man he wants to be, and every girl has a hero image that colors her idea of the man she wants to marry. Where do you think that image primarily comes from? It comes from you as a dad; that is a tall order. You do need God's constant help. Your love and praise are so crucial.

5. *Major on your marriage.* In Ephesians 5:28-29, Paul wrote, "In this same way, husbands ought to love their wives as their own bodies. He who loves his wife loves himself. After all, no one ever hated his own body, but he feeds and cares for it, just as Christ does the church" (NIV). Now here is a way the devil has twisted us totally around. I have a good friend in Atlanta who owns several Christian bookstores. He told me that a recent survey demonstrated that there are hundreds of Christian books on marriage, and more than two-thirds of the readers of those books are women—even the books addressed to men! Does that mean men don't care enough?

I talked to a man recently who sells insurance, and he could not wait to get to a clinic on selling more insurance. He was so motivated and excited. But this same man would not even consider looking at anything that would improve his marriage. He thinks he has a great home, but he has an emotionally starved wife.

The greatest thing your children can see is a man who believes marriage is so precious that he gives it his time. The one thing that will go a thousand miles to protect your children from divorce is you as a father demonstrating to them that your marriage is more important than your job.

I want to say something very daring with which you may not agree. But I am thoroughly convinced that it is biblically true. If your job endangers your family, if you are neglecting and harming them because of your job, your job ought to go—even if it means making less money. Because when you get to be seventy years old and you review your life, the only things that will matter will be your relationship to God and your relationship to your family.

6. Be the priest to your family. The final thing I want to share is in the area of spiritual leadership. You need to be the priest to your family—someone who represents them to God. Don't be afraid of that. Ephesians 6:4 says, "Fathers, do not exasperate your children; instead, bring them up in the training and instruction of the Lord" (NIV).

Recently, God revealed something very precious to me about this verse. It had never before hit me to whom God was speaking. He is talking to the *father,* not the mother. Again, I am not lowering the mother's responsibility in this area at all. But God puts the primary responsibility of spiritual training on the man. God has so programmed life, men, that you cannot help but be the spiritual leaders in your families. You may be a godless individual, but you will still lead them. You will just be leading them the wrong way. The majority of the time, the children in a family take on the moral and spiritual values of the father. That is a staggering responsibility and we need God's help.

The greatest success you as husband and father can have is to find a balance of achievement in every area. When you follow biblical standards, you need not sacrifice either your financial freedom nor your family. Make your dominant goal total success. Pray for God's wisdom as you build financial security, emotional stability, and spiritual prosperity for your wife and children.

NINE
POSITIVE THINKING AND NEGATIVE PEOPLE

When I first started doing crusades, Amy and I went to a community in northeastern Kentucky, and we were quite excited about the meetings to come. When I got there, the leader of the event said to me, "Ron, I'm sorry, but there are some very vicious rumors being circulated about you and Amy and the work you are doing." I asked him what he was talking about, and he responded, "Well, they say you've started a cult group, and you're another Jim Jones."

Since that time I have had to work through the opposition, disapproval, and sometimes the attacks of negative people who have tried to derail what Amy and I are doing in our ministry. They often think they are doing us good by criticizing our dream. You may discover as you talk about your dreams that you too will get negative, hostile opposition. People will misunderstand you, your dreams, your methods, and they will throw negative material in your face continually. My purpose in this chapter is to help you come to a definite freedom from negative people. I want to give you some principles that God has taught me in the last couple of years on how to handle this thorny problem. First we're going to take a look at positive thinking from a Christian perspective.

POSITIVE THINKING AND THE CHRISTIAN

Many conservative Christians feel that positive thinking is ungodly and humanistic. They fear that adopting a positive-thinking attitude will throw someone into a "human only" attitude—*your* strength, *your* confidence, *your* hard work—leaving out Jesus Christ. I'd like to communicate to these Christians what true positive thinking is all about.

There are two things that positive thinking is not. First, it is not a sacrifice of realism. A positive thinker's head is not in the clouds. He is not unrealistic; he is the most realistic person on earth. He isn't pretending that bad things aren't bad but believes instead that he is not going to be beaten by those bad things because of his positive attitude. Second, positive thinking is not a substitute for knowing Jesus Christ. He is the only doorway to God and I believe that with all my heart. Positive thinking is not a substitute faith.

So what is positive thinking? I stumbled onto

the greatest definition I have ever heard in a book by Earl Nightingale [*Earl Nightingale's Greatest Discovery* (Dodd-Mead, 1987)]. He said, "Positive thinking is looking at life with a cheerful expectation of happy results." And as a committed Christian, I choose to live this way.

Psychologists will tell you that the first ten to twenty minutes after waking up in the morning are crucial to the rest of your day. Those opening minutes set the tone. That means that you want to get started right! Imagine jumping out of bed, thinking about all of your opportunities, and then saying out loud, "I have a cheerful expectation of happy results today." Can you see the energy that releases? You don't want to shrivel up and die before the end of your life. You want a positive, cheerful expectation of happy results. Look at Proverbs 17:22: "A cheerful heart is good medicine, but a crushed spirit dries up the bones" (NIV). That's vivid language. And it's a right way to view life.

Humanistic vs. Christian Positive Thinking
There are five basic differences between humanistic and Christian positive thinking.

1. The roots of confidence. To the humanist, positive thinking is rooted entirely in yourself. All of your confidence in life is rooted totally in you. I talked to a self-made man once who was so proud that he didn't need God, a network of friends, his family, anyone—and then he got really sick. Suddenly this brave man who didn't need anybody wanted to find God, find friends, find help.

The difference in Christian positive thinking is obvious. Your confidence is rooted in God, in who he is, in the reliability of his principles. Christian positive thinking has solid values, a solid core. What if we really have a threat of nuclear war? As a committed Christian whose confidence is rooted in God, I don't have to be thrown into a blind panic, because God is beyond nuclear war, and his purposes will be fulfilled his way no matter what the Soviets or Americans do. My confidence, my happiness, my cheerfulness is rooted in something solid and dependable. It's powerful.

Romans 8:28 says, "And we know that in all things God works for the good of those who love him, who have been called according to his purpose" (NIV). What an incredible truth and confidence builder that is. When you get into a dark night of agony and doubt, it's good to know that God is working all of these things together for good. Psalm 48:14 says, "For this great God is our God forever and ever. He will be our guide until we die" (TLB). You're not making decisions alone. Pray and seek God's wisdom.

2. The focus of goals. For the humanistic positive thinker, all of his positive goals are this-life goals. It's all for this earth, right here and now. But the Christian positive thinker has goals beyond these goals. He doesn't quit when this life ends. That's a great reason to be positive!

3. The source of pride. The humanistic positive thinker promotes a self-destructive form of pride, whereas the Christian positive thinker has a proper awareness of his dependence on God as creator. Let me explain the difference here. One of the great dangers of success is success itself because you become puffed up with an exaggerated sense of your own importance. This can be self-destructive. A man I respect told me, "Ron, as God blesses you and you have more success, beware of the wrong kind of pride—the kind that suddenly doesn't need other counsel." The danger of destruction comes with this kind of arrogance. It will kill your success and your family relationships.

Christian positive thinking promotes a proper awareness of your need of God. There is a principle in the Bible that I call the weak-link principle: there are certain things the Bible warns you about—adultery, stealing, lust outside of marriage, the wrong kind of pride—because God knows that wherever your weak link is, that is where you can fall apart. Let God help you remember to watch that area because the forces against you will attack your weak link.

4. The view of man. Humanistic positive thinking is absolutely convinced that we are born basically good and just get better automatically. But the Christian positive thinker knows the truth: we need God's help. Unfortunately, in recent years our educational system has supported this humanistic philosophy, and it has become entrenched in the thinking of those around us. The only problem with this theory is that it doesn't explain human evil. If we are basically good, why do we do bad so often? The truth is that we were all born with a bent away from God. That's why God sent Jesus Christ to help us, to save us, to forgive us, and to make us right with a loving God who really wants our success.

5. *The view of death.* A humanistic positive thinker feels the end is the end. When he dies, it's over. The whole thing just stops. But for the Christian positive thinker life goes beyond this life. The Bible teaches that "no mere man has ever seen, heard or even imagined what wonderful things God has ready for those who love the Lord" (1 Corinthians 2:9, TLB).

So, Christians, you have things to be positive about! If anybody in the whole world ought to be positive, it is you. Life doesn't end for those who know Christ; it goes beyond. God is a God who wants to use you in a positive way. I love being a positive Christian. It's powerful.

NEGATIVE PEOPLE
As hard as you try to be positive, the cold water in the face comes from negative people. So let's look at the basic characteristics of negative people so you can recognize them anywhere.

1. *Disrespect.* The truly negative person is often rude to you. It may be your mother, your father-in-law, your boss, or the car dealership

man. I went into a grocery store in a little retirement town in Florida. There was a very sweet girl at the register, and I mentioned to her that closing time was near. She said, "Oh no it's not. Because in fifteen minutes a whole bunch of people will come in. They'll try to grab things off the shelf, and they'll be angry because they can't get things the way they want." Then she added, "I get so tired of all this retired rudeness." Some people have lived their whole lives like this—negative. The negative person continually communicates disrespect and rudeness.

2. Tension, worry, and fear. The negative person creates an atmosphere of tension, worry, and fear. If you challenge a negative person, telling him to look at something as positive, he'll respond by saying he is just trying to be realistic. He spreads gloom.

A few years ago Amy confronted me, saying, "You have become so wrapped up in working that you have become negative and critical at home. You drain me, and I can't be free because I live with you." You had better believe I started praying about that and asking God to help me with it. She was right. I was having a hard time during that period.

Negative people are almost addicted to worry. It's like a fix. Whenever a negative person faces difficulty, his tendency is to tighten up with tension. He expects the worse. He has lived negatively for so long that his negative attitudes give him a sense of security and control over his world. He is so comfortable with his usual negative response that he fears the attempt to become positive, although he may actually suspect the greater freedom that lies in a positive approach to life.

3. Dream and idea killers. A negative person really does want to kill your dreams and ideas, as shocking as that seems, as unfair as it is. He wants to keep you where you are. Yes, you love this person and care for him, but you have to realize that he is trying to kill your ideas like a big game hunter. On the surface he may be very polite to you—until you say you have a great idea or a big dream—and then he launches torpedoes to get you.

Why does the negative person kill your dreams? sabotage your hopes? Because he has adopted a small mind-set. He has a little approach to life. Everything is protected and cautious, and he wants to pull you down to that level with him.

4. Criticism. The negative person criticizes as a pattern. He doesn't criticize you on occasion but as a life-style. I know all of us need some correction now and then, but nobody needs constant criticism.

The education department at the college I attended was very negative. Their whole approach to educating educators was to criticize the living daylights out of them. The horrible truth was that a lot of the teachers teaching teachers to teach couldn't teach. They were dream stealers.

That's the way they lived.

5. Control. The objective of a negative person is control—controlling you. He may be an emotional bully, trying to intimidate you. Be careful not to fall into the negative person's trap of measuring yourself by his standards, because his standards are negative.

You can't stop being positive because a negative person tells you to. Why believe him? Your life message should be positive, not negative. You are going to improve the quality of your life. So why listen to what a negative person is saying? Don't do it.

I came across something in Proverbs that is such an amazing statement about negative people, I just sat there in awe. It's Proverbs 6:16-19, and it lists seven attitudes that God hates: (1) haughty eyes—acting as if you have a lot of status; (2) a lying tongue; (3) hands that shed innocent blood; (4) a heart that devises negative, wicked schemes; (5) feet that are quick to rush to evil; (6) a false witness who pours out lies; and (7) a person who stirs dissension among his family and friends.

Do you know why God hates all of those negative attitudes? Because God loves you. He hates the negative. He is a positive God. Now I do believe in a real heaven and a real hell. So, there are negatives in the Bible, but God himself is not a negative God. He's positive and he wants to build your success, and you can build it on a foundation of knowing him.

WHAT MAKES A NEGATIVE PERSON?

You are going to run into negative people all through your life. Why do people choose to be negative? Let me give you some reasons to help you understand them.

Unresolved Anger

You are going to meet people every day who are angry—and they may not know it. They are angry at their circumstances: they don't like their jobs, their cars, their homes. They don't like their situation, but they won't do anything to change it. Or they are angry at someone in their past, usually a parent. Where does unresolved anger come from? It has at its roots several things.

1. Jealousy. One root of unresolved anger is jealousy. A person with unresolved anger has lived his whole life jealous of somebody but he is unwilling to change or do anything about it. It's his choice, and then it comes out as negativism.

A few years ago, while I was working on a master's degree, Amy and I went to a rural community in Illinois to do a two-week crusade with rallies and meetings. The person coordinating the event had us stay in his home since there was no hotel in the area. During our time there we saw a number of people come to know Jesus Christ; the meetings were good. But about four or five days into the crusade, something very ugly began to happen. Our host, a pastor and community leader, became increasingly difficult to work with. He said insulting things to us and made cutting remarks. After about two or three days of this, I decided to confront him, and he got even more negative. He told us how awful we were, how our motivation was wrong, how the meetings had been very unsuccessful. I couldn't figure out what had provoked this change. We had been polite, had built him up in the community, and had done all of the right things sincerely.

A few days later, the man made a remark that explained all of it. With real venom in his voice, he said to me, "You know what the real problem is? You are going to that school and you are getting another degree." And he walked out. I made some inquiries of others and found out that this guy had not graduated from college. My education was a real problem for him. The fact that I was earning a graduate degree ripped his guts out; he couldn't stand it.

So there will be times when you are dealing with people who are negative because of sheer jealousy.

2. *Disappointments.* A person can become angry and hostile when he allows every disappointment to poison him a little bit more. He may try to blame someone for that. Let's face facts with maturity right now. You will go through disappointments, but the secret to your success will be how you respond when your disappointments come. Robert Schuller has a great quote: "Bad things happen to everybody. The difference is

your response. Your response will determine whether you become better or you become bitter. It's up to you" (*Move Ahead with Possibility Thinking* [Revell, 1973]).

I met a man in Indianapolis who was angry because his eighty-year-old father had died a year before. He blamed God for his father's death. His mom told me, "My son has always been a negative person. As a child he made the decision to allow everything that happens that he doesn't like to poison him."

Sometimes sympathy is the worst thing you can do for somebody. There are times when a person needs to stand on his own two feet and grow up. Now I'm not addressing those who are facing real tragedy but rather those who allow every disappointment in life to rule and dominate them. This will lead to unresolved anger.

3. *Battered dignity.* Unresolved anger comes because someone has experienced battered dignity. He's been slapped around by somebody. His dignity as a person has been damaged.

I was in a store one Christmas and witnessed a man yelling at the top of his voice to his wife, "Hey, big mouth!" His wife jumped and turned at the sound of her husband's voice. He laughed and said, "I knew you would answer to that." I watched the woman's eyes and saw a flicker of pain. She didn't like to be embarrassed by this emotional bully to whom she happened to be married. Some people become negative because they get slapped around.

4. Early insult. The next reason for unresolved anger is when there has been an experience of early insult. I was in a huge department store in Florida where I saw a young mother and her little girl, who was becoming restless. The mother was fed up and pushed away the cart in which the little girl sat, saying, "I don't want you anymore. I don't want you anymore. Go away. Go away." This is an extreme example, but what negative thing did someone tell you as a child that you have never forgotten? I remember a relative of mine saying to me that I would always be fat. Now, I'm not slim, but I don't think I'm fat. But because of what I was told, I have a hard time thinking otherwise. When the insult comes from an authority figure of any kind—Mom, Dad, teacher, pastor—the child tends to accept it as truth. The child can't discriminate between what's true and what's not. So when it comes from an authority figure, it begins to damage self-esteem, anger is produced, and the person can become negative.

5. Deep inferiority. A person becomes negative person when he has such a deep sense of inferiority that it becomes what psychologists call free-floating hostility. Have you ever watched people in traffic, at a stoplight, at a grocery store—and seen the angry way they deal with others? You are around people constantly who are trying to prove themselves.

Feelings of inferiority are rooted in early negative experiences. The ego is battered; self-esteem is challenged. Self-doubt is planted deep in the personality. All of this combines to create a sense of powerlessness, which then becomes anger. This unresolved anger seeks an acceptable outlet—often targeted at other people.

Cover-up for Failure

The second reason why someone is negative is to cover-up his failures. It's a smokescreen. He will tell you with great conviction why things can't be done because he isn't doing them. He will then tell you why *you* can't do something, producing his excuses in advance.

1. Responsibility shifter. The negative person tends to be a responsibility shifter: he blames everybody else for his failures. Dexter Yager, a businessman I truly respect, said the one word he wants to communicate to people today is *responsibility.* People have to take responsibility for their own lives, their own successes, and their own failures. The first time you hear something like that, you tend to rebel and reject it because you want excuses for your failures. They want to blame someone or something, but the real root is that you fail because at some point it is your fault, and you succeed because you made the right choices. Now, I am not saying that every bad thing that happens to you is your fault. What I am saying is if you are not succeeding and achieving, then you are responsible for it. *You are always a product of your choices.* The negative person rejects that responsibility.

2. Laziness. A negative person may be trying to cover up his laziness. A negative person will give you a hundred reasons why he can't build a dream, but it's usually because he is a lazy person. You may not feel that laziness is a big problem in America because you imagine somebody getting out of bed early in the morning, taking a shower, and heading off to his job, never thinking of himself as lazy. But he is because all he wants to do is let somebody else rule his life for him. All he wants to do is go to work, do the minimum it takes to keep the job, watch the clock, and live for the weekends—a lazy person.

You need to have an executive mentality. You should work because it is your business, your dream, your goal. You should work without complaint, without groaning. You should be willing to do the work. Many people reject this thinking because they are trained to be employees. You need to learn to think differently. The Bible is full of verses about the lazy man and the hard worker, especially in the book of Proverbs.

3. Superstitious speech. The negative person often believes in superstitious speech. He is so intensely afraid that awful things will happen to him that he talks about them to ward them off. He talks about doom and disaster, about what he fears is going to happen: cancer, heart attacks, car wrecks. Speech becomes superstitious to him. You have to help this person realize that when he talks negative, he produces negative. The goal is to live right, trust God, have good health, and live free and positive.

4. Sidetrack from the truth. A negative person may cover up his failures by using negativism to sidetrack you from the truth. A wife may respond negatively to her husband's idea for a new business venture and tell him he can't do it. But the real reason she is down on the idea is that she is lazy and doesn't want to do the extra work needed to help him. She hopes to sidetrack him by her negative comments so that she doesn't have to tell him the real reason.

Emotional Weakness

Negative people are often negative because of emotional wimpiness and weakness. The emotionally wimpy person tends to have an exaggerated belief in the power of his enemies to win; he panics easily. The enemy could be anything, and this person believes that everybody else is more powerful than he is. He lacks strength and courage and lives a life of fear. Charles Swindoll, a great Christian leader and author, says in *The Quest for Character* (Multnomah, 1987) that people have to be trained to stop their passive self-pity and change it into active courage. A few characteristics of the emotionally weak person follow.

1. Lack of emotional discipline. You are going to deal with people all the time who are emotionally undisciplined. Why do I say undisciplined? A person who gives in to fear easily is choosing defeat. You can choose to be emotionally disciplined and say no to the fear.

2. Faulty view of life. An emotionally weak person has a faulty way of looking at life. He sees through negative lenses and expects the worst. I recently read a great book about World War II, and the chapter on the Jewish holocaust made quite an impact on me. The Jews were stripped totally naked to humiliate and embarrass them and made to lie in pits while they were machine-gunned to death. And that was one of the easier ways they had to die. After reading this I thought about those negative, wimpy people who complain about everything in life, whose perspective on life is that if the heat turns on they give up. Most of us don't know anything about suffering, and I thought, "God help me not to sweat all this petty stuff. Help me realize what some people have gone through for freedom and for dignity."

3. Victim mentality. Emotionally wimpy people tend to have a victim mentality. They see themselves as victims and feel that everybody is abusing them. We have so many people that are self-centered with a me, me, me attitude.

Domination

Negative people often have a drive to dominate other people by putting them down. This shows up in the person who exhibits a phony intellectualism. He drops big words and is very arrogant. I know someone who can't get into a conversation without dominating it, trying to intimidate the other person. At the heart of phony intellectualism is deep insecurity. This person can't let you have any dreams and usually is not accomplishing anything significant himself. This takes another form in verbal intimidation. The negative person wants you to feel that you don't know anything.

Need to Hurt

Lastly, the reason some people are negative is they have a neurotic need to hurt you. I wish it weren't true, but occasionally you will run into someone like this. Why? Because at some point he was hurt. This isn't an excuse, but it does help you understand him. If you are that kind of person, remember two things: you can never eliminate your hurt by hurting other people, and you must turn to God and let him heal your hurt through Jesus Christ. He can heal your hurts.

LIVING WITH NEGATIVE PEOPLE

By now you may be pretty discouraged because you feel that changing the negative person you love is a monumental task. So, I want to give you some solid, helpful information: you can't change him, but you can change yourself.

1. Be realistic. The negative person has made a choice to be negative. You cannot force the positive onto him. There is no magic button you can push, no right combination of words that will make him want to change. You can't love him just the right way. He is determined to be negative and to change your positive into a negative. So be realistic and realize that it is not your job to force change on your negative person.

2. Don't let him spoil your success. You need to decide that you will refuse to allow anyone else to spoil your success. We live in a generation where emotions rule: you are helpless to change the way you feel. But we can't live our lives on feelings. Emotions are unreliable. So even if somebody works hard to make you feel negative, you don't have to accept it. You have the power of emotional choice.

Proverbs 14:7 says, "Stay away from a foolish man, for you will not find knowledge on his lips" (NIV). Don't have emotional involvement with that type of person. Later I am going to deal with having a spouse who is negative.

3. Be your own best friend. Love yourself enough not to become an ally to your enemies. Why believe them? It is your choice again. Proverbs 13:20 says, "Be with wise men and become wise. Be with evil men and become evil" (TLB). Whoever you allow to influence you is your responsibility. Some of you continue to allow a negative person to influence you, and he is spoiling your success. Do something about that relationship.

Proverbs 22:24-25 has some positive principles. "Keep away from angry, short-tempered men, lest you learn to be like them and endanger your soul" (TLB). The Bible says not to make friends with an angry man. You don't have to allow negative people to call the shots in your emotional life.

4. Choose what you talk about. Proverbs 19:27 says, "Stop listening to teaching that contradicts what you know is right" (TLB). In other words, stop learning from material that causes you to believe things that are not the truth. Watch what you talk about, whom you talk about, and the way you talk.

Dr. Charles Stanley, a man I love and respect tremendously, said to me on one occasion, "Ron, the secret of victory and defeat in your life is as close to you as your own tongue." Your conversation has power. I challenge you to keep track of the way you speak for a few days by using a journal or tape recorder. You will probably be amazed at what you discover about your own conversational weaknesses. You have to decide to speak positively about people and situations. When you speak positively, you begin to change.

I say two things to myself every morning when I get up. First I quote Psalm 118:24: "This is the day the Lord has made. [I] will rejoice and be glad in it" (TLB). And then I quote what Earl Nightingale said: "Today I am going to live with a cheerful expectation of happy results." And my subconscious says, "Hey guys, he has given us our instructions for today." That may sound crazy to you, but it works. Your subconscious mind listens to what you say verbally and begins to do what you say.

162

The Bible says in Proverbs 15:1, "A gentle answer turns away wrath" (TLB). If someone speaks negatively or angrily to you, and you respond in a loving and kind way, you can defuse the situation before it explodes. Proverbs 15:4 says, "The tongue that brings healing is a tree of life" (NIV). You ought also to make a commitment that you will become an encourager. And when you do this, you are automatically encouraged in the process. Build others up. You have so much power in your relationships by what you say.

5. *Put on positive, protective armor.* Protect what goes into your mind. Saul Bellow, an American author, was quoted in *The Closing of the American Mind* (Allan Bloom [Simon & Schuster, 1987]) as saying, "Everybody lives in a thought-world." It is crucial to populate your thought-world with positive material.

You also need the right models and mentors in your life. Learn from people you respect, whose lives you want to copy. The Bible says in Proverbs 1:5, "A wise man will hear and increase learning, and a man of understanding will attain wise counsel" (NKJV). What you think about will change your life, and that's a guarantee.

VICTORY OVER NEGATIVISM

When Amy and I first got married, I had a physically violent temper. I never struck or harmed Amy, but I damaged our apartment. One time we were going two hours away to visit my mother for her birthday and Amy was having final exams in college. She had worked late into the night and then got up at 4:00 A.M. to bake my mother a cake. We got into the car and I got really angry about something. I had a warped idea that that was how you handled situations if you were a man. Amy held the cake as we drove away, and we were discussing something really petty, and I got angry again. I did my usual thing and tried to find something to break or smash. So I hit the brakes really hard, the car came to a quick halt, and the cake went smashing onto the windshield. The chocolate oozed onto the seat. My wife just sat there, looked at the cake, looked at me, and began to weep. God ripped something out of me at that point. And I thought, "Oh, God, you have got to teach me how to change."

I have undergone some immense changes in the last few years, and I wrote down a list of the reasons I have been able to change in this and other areas.

1. *Sincere desire to please God.* I have been able to change because at the heart of my life is a totally sincere desire to please God. And it didn't come because I had a religious family. I never went to church until I was in my teens. I didn't even know what was in the Bible. I knew nothing spiritually, but a man shared with me how to know Jesus Christ personally. It wasn't emotional. I just asked Jesus Christ to come into my life, and I accepted his death on the cross. There was implanted in me an intense

desire to please God and it has never left. It has weakened at times, but it has never left.

2. Desire to be my best. I also have built into me a real desire to be my best. My mom and dad did this—not to make me a perfectionist—but to encourage me to be my best.

3. Expose hidden agendas. I have been able to change because of a willingness to expose hidden agendas in my life. When Amy would make plans, I always would have secret plans of my own. I would maneuver and manipulate the situation to get what I wanted, but I would do it in such a way that I would try to let her think that it wasn't I doing it. I always had a hidden agenda, and it wasn't until several years ago that God brought me to a point where I had to choose honesty.

4. My wife, Amy. Amy has always told me the truth, but she has done it wrapped in complete love and unconditional loyalty to me. I believe that is what has made it work for me. Her truth is hard truth. My wife never lets me off the hook when I am wrong. She tells me straight out, on target; she minces no words, and I thank God for that because I fight the truth knowing in the depths of my soul that Amy is right.

5. Logic rather than emotion. I have always had a willingness to be persuaded by logic rather than follow my own emotions. That means that I have accepted logic even when I didn't want to hear it.

6. Desire for respect. With all my heart I want

one crucial thing from my wife and my daughter: I want their respect. That is one of the major reasons I have been able to change. I want to earn it. I want them to respect me. I want that enough that I am willing to change.

7. Children. I don't want my children carrying negative baggage because of their dad. I can't and won't allow that.

I decided a long time ago that if any change were necessary in our marriage, I couldn't demand it from Amy. I had to give it myself. I believe that is part of family leadership, men. If there is a change needed in your marriage, you lead the change.

MARRIED TO A NEGATIVE PERSON

If you are married to someone who has really hurt you, or you have been really hurt by a friend or parent, consider trying these four things:

1. Get God's help. He's supernatural and can help you.

2. Stop being a victim. Don't feel sorry for yourself. Stop living in personal pity.

3. Forgive the negative person. This is done by choice and not emotion. You may also need to ask the negative person to forgive you if you have turned negative against him.

4. Go on with your life. You can't wallow in the past or the "has beens."

There is great power in positive thinking and

living, the power of a positive God and his Son. You have the power to *choose* how you are going to respond to life. Some of you may be the negative person I have described. I was, and it has been incredibly hard for me to change because I have had to go against my natural, negative tendencies. But if you have those negative tendencies, I hope and pray you will ask a loving God to help you change them and help you become a whole, healthy, positive person. You can be a bright example of a spiritually right, emotionally healthy, person, and there is no more urgent need than that in this day.

EPILOGUE
KNOWING GOD

The deepest need of your life is to know God. But is God knowable? If you can know him, what is it like? Is it scary? envigorating? unnerving? relaxing? What is it really like?

The God of the Bible is knowable and wants to be known. The only door to that knowledge is through a personal surrender to Jesus Christ as Savior. And beyond that door lies the greatest of human adventures: to actually know God.

Our society is confused largely because it is cut off from God. Men and women are like children in search of a reliable way home but who worry that the home doesn't even exist. The answer to society's search is to know God.

What about your own search? You may be from a traditional Christian background. You may have made a sincere commitment to Jesus Christ. You may even attend church frequently. But how real is God to you? For you God may be lost in the complex world of religious rules. You have been pounded by guilt. Deep within you dread God. He seems to suck the joy out of your life. To know him is your great desire, but to know him is also your great fear.

I want you to stop your worry. Breathe easy. Relax. The God of the Bible wants to be your *heavenly Father.* He wants to help you defeat negative habits. He wants to release you from the control of self-centered sin. He wants to fulfill your life. You are important to him. He wants to know you. He wants you to know him. I suggest you do three things:

1. Read carefully in a modern translation the book of Genesis—the Old Testament account of the beginning for all of us. Then read the book of Psalms—the Old Testament book of how to show love and affection to God. Next read the book of John—the New Testament presentation of why Jesus came; and then the book of Philippians—a New Testament book about how to enjoy Jesus Christ.

2. Every morning when you wake up, hurry to get alone with God and tell him how much you love him and how happy you are that he loves you.

3. Try hard to help people understand how very much God loves them.

If you do not already know God and have a personal relationship with Jesus Christ, I'd like to encourage you to take that step. I assure you that it will be the beginning toward healing all the areas we've looked at in this book and many more as well. Your life cannot be whole without it.

You must first recognize your need for God. The Bible says, "All have sinned; all fall short of God's glorious ideal" (Romans 3:23, TLB). We *all* need God.

The next step is to confess your sin to God. Admit to him that you need his gift of salvation. "But if we confess our sins to him, he can be depended on to forgive us and to cleanse us from every wrong. [And it is perfectly proper for God to do this for us because Christ died to wash away our sins]" (1 John 1:9, TLB).

And finally, you need to accept Jesus Christ as your Savior. "To all who received him [Jesus Christ], he gave the right to become children of God. All they needed to do was to trust him to save them" (John 1:12, TLB).

God provided a way for you to know him and to have a relationship with him because he loves you. "For God loved the world so much that he gave his only Son so that anyone who believes in him shall not perish but have eternal life" (John 3:16, TLB).

Nothing can replace your personal knowledge of God. The pieces of your life will fit only with him at the core. Why not take this step now—and begin the exciting adventure of knowing and loving God? Learn to really love the God who really loves you.

ACKNOWLEDGMENTS

Acknowledgments are more than a necessary courtesy; they represent the vital contributions of important people to an author's thoughts.

I have never met a greater man than Dexter Yager. His support and that of his wife, Birdie, have been monumental. His influence on my life continues to be profound and pervasive.

I sincerely thank Cliff Johnson and Ellen Parks of Tyndale House Publishers for practical and editorial assistance. Their aid was essential.

Richard and Andrea Shupert have been catalysts whose original encouragement got the book off the ground. Andrea also contributed the title.

Bill and Peggy Florence, Terry and Sandy Thoms, and Ken and Shirley Goss added friendship and support at key moments. I am also deeply grateful for the indispensable support of Pat and Linda Cahill.

My own understanding of the dynamics of a spiritually and emotionally healthy family has been built on the insights of my dear friends Dr. Charles Stanley and Dr. David Seamands. Their leadership is remarkable.

Doyle Yager has poured his talent into this project. We have succeeded at least partially because of him.

God has taught me my greatest lessons through my wife, Amy, and my daughter, Allison. My family happiness flows from them.

Mom and Dad, I love you—thank you for my home as a child.

Ron Ball

The principles of family life I have shared with Ron have not come overnight. It has been a process—a journey—of trial and error. I have earnestly sought God's will and equally tried to do the best I could with his help. I have watched others and learned from them. I have also tried to analyze the action and reaction of parents as well as children. I have seven children and nine grandchildren, and I know what worked with me as a child, and learned what worked as a parent and now a grandparent.

I would like to thank my parents, Leonard and Gertrude Yager, Sr., for helping to mold me as a child and then as a young adult in order that I might be the person I was meant to be.

My thanks and appreciation go out to my wife, Birdie, for her loyalty to me and her commitment to our children when I had to be away for extended business trips.

Additional thanks go to my brothers and sisters: Richard, Ella, Lillian, and Leonard, Jr.

I would sincerely like to thank my children: Dexter, Jr., and Doyle (the twins), April, Lisa, Jeff, Leanne, and Steven.

I want to extend my personal thanks to Dr. Charles Stanley for the Godly influence he has had on Ron's life. Dr. Stanley's leadership and training have helped Ron and me to build a relationship of trust. Ron has trusted my leadership, direction, and advice; and I in turn have trusted Ron to research and develop subjects we have discussed at great length, which he has delivered to my network of business people.

Dexter Yager, Sr.